The
Evolution of the Messianic Idea

THE EVOLUTION
OF THE
MESSIANIC IDEA

A Study in Comparative Religion

By the Rev.

W. O. E. OESTERLEY, D.D.

Jesus College, Cambridge.

*Joint Author, with G. H. Box, M.A., of
"The Religion and Worship of the Synagogue."*

Eugene, Oregon

Wipf and Stock Publishers
199 West 8th Avenue, Suite 3
Eugene, Oregon 97401

The Evolution of the Messianic Idea
A Study in Comparative Religion
By Oesterley, W.O.E.
ISBN: 1-59244-699-X
Publication date 5/19/2004
Previously published by Sir Isaac Pitman and Sons, 1908

PREFATORY NOTE.

THE following *Dissertation* was accepted as sufficient for the degree of *Doctor of Divinity* in the University of Cambridge.

In its present form the work differs slightly from that in which it was originally presented. The author desires to express his thanks to the Divinity Professors for having permitted him to make the following alterations :

> All Hebrew quotations have been translated, and isolated Hebrew words either transliterated or translated ; all quotations from classical writings, as well as those from modern French and German works, have likewise been translated.

By this means it was thought that the book might be made more acceptable to the general reader.

In dealing with a subject which covers such a wide area as the " Messianic Idea," it is impossible always to give reasons for statements which are made ; a certain amount of knowledge on the part of the reader must be assumed. Moreover, to attempt a detailed exposition of all the reasons

PREFATORY NOTE

for holding certain views would manifestly take up a great deal of valuable space, often unnecessarily; this would especially be the case when, as here, such reasons can be gathered from the general argument of the book. So that if it should sometimes appear in the following pages that things are somewhat dogmatically expressed, the writer trusts that this will not be put down to a wrong motive on his part; he is too fully sensible of the many considerations involved in every large question to imagine that final conclusions are easily reached.

The subject to be treated of touches upon many highly controversial topics, in regard to which a very large variety of opinion exists; even upon the central thought itself of the book, as expressed in the title, many readers will, no doubt, differ *in toto* from the writer. Yet it was not, truly, with any idea of controversy that the subject was chosen. The whole cycle of conceptions embraced in the term "Messianism" had presented great difficulties to the writer, and in trying to explain to himself the How and Why of it all, a partial solution, at all events, seemed to him to be found in the mental constitution of men, and the facts of human history. The fact of the former being of divine creation and the latter, in general, of divine guidance, does not preclude the belief that the development of the one and the course of the other

PREFATORY NOTE

is to a large extent conditioned by man's free-will; so that though Messianism was of divine origin, man had his part to play in its evolution. This, as will be seen more fully later on, seemed to explain some of the problems connected with the subject, and thus to some extent to remove the difficulties of belief which it presented.

It is the sincere hope of the writer that the following pages may be of some use to those who have perhaps been brought face to face with the difficulties which he has experienced.

W. O. E. O.

April, 1908.

CONTENTS.

PART I.

THE ANTECEDENTS OF THE MESSIANIC IDEA.

CHAPTER I.

INTRODUCTION . . . p. 1

CHAPTER II.

THE EARLIEST FORMS OF MYTH DUE TO ELEMENTAL CHARACTERISTICS IN MAN.

Some elemental characteristics in primitive man considered: (i) Superstitious fear, owing to animistic conceptions; (ii) The sense of dependence on a higher power; (iii) The desire to be happy—Primitive man, in giving articulate expression to these elemental characteristics, framed some of the earliest forms of myth. . . . . p. 19

CHAPTER III.

FLOATING MYTH-MATERIAL WAS USED BY OLD TESTAMENT WRITERS AND ADAPTED TO HIGHER TEACHING.

For the present purpose only a restricted number of myths come into consideration—In the case of these single original forms are not to be postulated, since they are the expression of human characteristics all the world over—The three myths to be examined; those of (i) A primeval cruel monster who became identified with the watery element; (ii) A divine-human Hero who saved men from the monster, and brought them material blessings; (iii) A happy time long ago—A floating myth-material was utilized by some of the Old Testament writers, and adapted to more spiritual uses—In their *Hebrew* form these three myths may be designated: (i) The "Tehom-myth"; (ii) The "Jahwe-myth"; (iii) The "Paradise-myth." . . . p. 29

CONTENTS

CHAPTER IV.

THE "TEHOM-MYTH."

THIS myth embodies the belief of which the root-idea is the existence of a primeval cruel monster who was identified with the principle of "evil," *i.e.*, harmfulness—Its Hebrew form is spiritualized, though antique *traits* are still clearly discernible; it represents, therefore, an echo rather than the original voice. . . . . . . p. 41

CHAPTER V.

THE "TEHOM-MYTH" AMONG THE HEBREWS.

EXAMINATION of Biblical passages: Gen. i. 2, ii. 4 ff.; Amos ix. 3*b*; Isa. xxx. 7; Isa. xxvii. 1; Isa. li. 9. 10; Ps. lxxiv. 12-15; Ps. lxxxix. 9-11; Job xxvi. 12, 13; Job xl. 25-xli. 26. These passages are not exhaustive, but are intended to serve as examples. . . . . . . p. 45

CHAPTER VI.

THE "TEHOM-MYTH" AMONG OTHER PEOPLES.

THE underlying idea of the "Tehom-myth" among the Hebrews is paralleled by other forms of this myth among many peoples; this justifies the inference that in the Old Testament we have but one of the many expressions of a root-conception which is common to man—Examples of other forms of the "Tehom-myth": Chaldæan, Phœnician, Egyptian, Zoroastrian, Greek, Algonquin, Iroquois, South American, Mexican, African, Peruvian—This list is far from being exhaustive. . . . . . p. 59

CHAPTER VII.

EXTENSIONS OF THE "TEHOM-MYTH."

THERE are reasons for believing that in the Old Testament there are to be found two "extensions" of the "Tehom-myth," viz.: (i) The Story of the Fall; (ii) The Story of the Flood—In the latter the myth of "Tehom-Rabbah" is to be differentiated from the legend, based on fact, of the Flood (*Hammabbūl*). . . . . . p. 75

CONTENTS

CHAPTER VIII.
THE " JAHWE-MYTH."

A MORE appropriate name would be "Saviour-myth" or "*Heilbringer*-myth"—The original form of the myth—The "Heilbringer" a Hero who overcame the primeval watery monster, and who also brought temporal blessings to his people—Some Old Testament passages considered: Gen. ii. 5-7, 19; Isa. li. 9-11; Ps. lxv. 7, 8; Ps. lxxiv. 12-17; Ps. lxxxix. 6-19; Ps. civ. 5-9—These passages, again, are only examples. . . . . p. 83

CHAPTER IX.
THE " JAHWE(*HEILBRINGER*)-MYTH " AMONG OTHER PEOPLES.

THE underlying conception of the "Jahwe-myth" not the exclusive possession of the Hebrews—Examples of "*Heilbringer*-myths": Babylonian, Egyptian, Indian, Zoroastrian, Greek, Algonquin, Iroquois, Thlinkeet, Bakaïri, Namaqua, Zulu, Bushmen, Zuñi, Mayas, Ahts—These only a few examples out of a great many that exist— The "Heilbringer" a personality who is half-human, half-divine. . . . . . . p. 108

CHAPTER X.
THE " PARADISE-MYTH."

ONE conception underlies all forms of the "Paradise-myth"—Usually it consists of two parts, a past and a future, which did not originally exist together—The supposed steps by which this myth was arrived at—Some Biblical passages considered: Gen. ii. 8-iii.; Ps. xlviii. 2-4; Ezek. xxviii. 13-15; Isa. ii. 2-4 (=Mic. iv. 1-3); Isa. xi. 1-9; Isa. xxxv. 1-10—Inferences to be drawn from these passages. p. 123

CHAPTER XI.
THE " PARADISE-MYTH " AMONG OTHER PEOPLES.

THE *raison d'être* of this myth probably varied in different ages, but the main and original idea which gave birth to it remained constant all through—Different forms of the myth considered: Babylonian, Phœnician, Arab, Egyptian, Zoroastrian, Greek, Roman, Algonquin, Sioux, Gallas, Akwapim—These, again, are only a few examples of a great number. . . . . p. 140

CONTENTS

PART II.

SOME EXAMPLES OF ADAPTATION AND DEVELOPMENT.

CHAPTER XII.

SUMMARY OF THE MATERIAL DEALT WITH.

THE contents of the foregoing chapters summarized, and the salient points emphasized—Attempt to show that in the three myths considered above a logical sequence is discernible—With the later development of these myths, this thought-sequence tended to become obscured, and an intermixture between them gradually arose—Signs of this process probably to be seen in some Old Testament passages—Links in the history of the development of ideas become lost in transmission—These facts must be allowed for in studying the adaptation and development of the three myths under consideration. . . . . p. 161

CHAPTER XIII.

SATAN.

THE meaning of this word in the Old Testament; the difference in meaning in the older and later literature; suggested theory as to the reason of this difference—Further considerations: correspondence between the characteristics of *Tehom* and Satan; the prophetical teaching concerning the personality of God, and consequent development of the sense of sin; growing perception of the meaning of opposition to God—*Tehom*, the embodiment of harmfulness, developed into Satan, the embodiment of the principle of evil—Adaptation of earlier material, with some examples from pseudepigraphic literature, etc.—Theories as to the original of evil and its existence in the world; the "Yetser hara' "—The end of *Tehom* (Satan) predicted—The final development of the "Tehom-myth " in the *Apocalypse*.

p. 175

CONTENTS

CHAPTER XIV.

THE MESSIAH.

THE use and meaning of the word "Messiah" in the Old Testament—The examination of some Biblical passages in which the ancient "Heilbringer" conception appears to have been adapted and applied to the Messiah—Signs of development—Isa. ii. 2-4*a*; Isa. iv. 2-6—The "Branch of Jahwe"—The doctrine of the "Remnant"—Isa. ix. 5, 6.
p. 190

CHAPTER XV.

THE MESSIAH (CONTINUED).

"WONDERFUL-COUNSELLOR" — "Mighty-God" — "Father-Everlasting" — "Prince-of-Peace" — Messianic Teaching in pre-Christian times reaches its zenith in the book of Isaiah—Isa. xi. 1-5—The outpouring of the Divine Spirit—Summary of the Isaianic teaching. . . p. 212

CHAPTER XVI.

THE MESSIANIC ERA.

THE meaning of the phrase "The Day of Jahwe"—The prophetical conception of this "Day" contrasted with the popular conception—Further development of ideas concerning this "Day"—Some examples of adaptation and development of the "Golden Age" myth: its peaceful character; a time of happiness and contentment—The "Mount of God"—The "River of Life"—The "Tree of Life." . . . . p. 240

CHAPTER XVII.

CONCLUSION. . . p. 268

The Evolution of the Messianic Idea.

CHAPTER I.

INTRODUCTION.

THE expression "Messianic Idea," as here used, is intended to embrace the various conceptions which centre round the Person of the Messiah. Of these the main ones are, besides that concerning the Messiah Himself, the annihilation of the powers of evil, and, in consequence, the establishment of the Messianic rule of righteousness, justice and peace, and the resultant happiness of the subjects of this kingdom. These conceptions, as presented to us in the Bible, show distinct signs of having gone through an evolutionary process; this may be seen most plainly of all by comparing the Messianic picture as seen in the New Testament with that found in the Old Testament. But in the Old Testament there are many signs, some of which will be pointed out in the following pages, which indicate the existence of antecedent ideas concerning Messianic teaching; that is to say, that the evolutionary process is not restricted in its working to the Old

THE EVOLUTION OF THE MESSIANIC IDEA

and New Testaments, but that behind the former there is a history, a very long history indeed, of what for convenience' sake we term "Messianism." And to understand the great significance, in all its bearings, of Messianic teaching, it is indispensable that it should be considered, as far as this is possible, in its earliest beginnings. In the words, the truth of which is coming to be more and more realized, of the late Professor Robertson Smith : "To understand the ways of God with man, and the whole meaning of His plan of salvation, it is necessary to go back and see His work in its beginnings, examining the rudimentary stages of the process of revelation."[1] Many, even at the present day, are prepared to maintain, in opposition to these words, that there can be no such things as "rudimentary stages" in the process of revelation, because the idea of Revealed Religion implies something which, as far as it goes, is complete ; thus, they would say, for example, that the revelation on Mount Sinai did not admit of previous stages, because it was full and complete in itself. The study of Comparative Religion shows, however, that an attitude of this kind is untenable ; a whole world of facts cries out against such a supposed restriction of the divine activity among men to a particular

[1] *The Old Testament in the Jewish Church*, p. 192 (1895).

DIVINE ACTIVITY ETERNAL

period of the world's history. The special revelation, for example, in the Person of Jesus Christ, is the climax of what thinking men from the first dawn of understanding were feeling for and, no doubt unconsciously, looking forward to. It is, therefore, true to say that there were rudimentary stages of a belief in Christ during untold ages before men saw Him in the flesh; it is also true to say that Messianic prophecy in the Old Testament by no means exhausts all that was surging in men's minds concerning Him that was to come. It is difficult to doubt that St. Paul included all mankind when, in addressing the Athenians, he spoke of those who "should seek God, if haply they might feel after Him, and find Him, though He is not far from each one of us; for in Him we live and move, and have our being;"[1] with this St. Peter's words to Cornelius are in entire agreement: "Of a truth I perceive that God is no respecter of persons; but in every nation he that feareth Him and worketh righteousness is acceptable to Him."[2] It is not possible for a believer to conceive of a time during which God's interest in His highest creation was not actively shown forth; and therefore it must be the fact that untold millenniums ago, as soon as thought became articulate in man, the Spirit of God was

[1] Acts xvii. 27, 28.
[2] Acts x. 34, 35.

THE EVOLUTION OF THE MESSIANIC IDEA

working, and, as far as the very limited capacity of human beings permitted, revealing Himself in their hearts. When Dr. Farnell truly remarks that the study of Religion has shown "that all through the present societies of savage men there prevails an extraordinary uniformity, in spite of much local variation, in ritual and mythology, a uniformity so striking as to suggest belief in an ultimately identical tradition, or, perhaps more reasonably, the psychologic theory that the human brain-cell in different races at the same stage of development responds with the same religious speech or the same religious act to the same *stimuli* supplied by its environment,"[1] one may add that, whether tradition, it must in the last instance go back to some divine promptings of which primitive man made the best use that he was able, or whether environment, it must have been such as was brought about by the Creator of all things. Always and everywhere the Divine Mind has been at work—this, at least, must be the conviction of those who believe in the existence of a Divine Personality, Who has existed from all eternity, and by Whose creative act the Universe and all that it contains came to be. By saying this, the intention is far from wishing to deny a very special place to the Hebrew genius and to the literature of the Old Testament which,

[1] *The Evolution of Religion*, p. 9.

MEANING OF EVOLUTION

under God, it produced ; only the fact needs emphasis that the divine activity among men cannot, in view of our greater knowledge of God and of His Creation, nowadays be believed to have been restricted (in pre-Christian times) to the Israelite nation ; indeed, one of the objects of the following pages is to try and show that the testimony of the Old Testament itself is against such a belief ; and one of the most important factors in the evidence for this is the existence of just that " Messianic Idea " which is to form the subject of our present inquiry.

When one speaks of Evolution in connexion with a religious subject such as the " Messianic Idea," which, as must be obvious, involves the study of Comparative Religion, there are two special dangers which are ever-present, and against which it is very necessary to guard oneself. The first of these is the danger of using the word Evolution in a wrong way ; what has often been in the present writer's mind is so succinctly and plainly put by Dr. Illingworth, in his most recent work, that a few quotations from this may be permitted. " All true evolution is the gradual unfolding of a germ, and is characterized by unbroken continuity. . . . Evolution is merely a method, and originates and can originate nothing. Whatever we find existing at the end of an evolutionary process must have existed potentially,

THE EVOLUTION OF THE MESSIANIC IDEA

that is to say in germ, at its beginning. . . .
The fact is, that in becoming popular the conception of evolution has become very vague, and is commonly supposed to cover much more ground than is actually the case. . . . The seed which we describe as a potential tree or flower is packed with that potentiality from the beginning of its existence, and its component atoms are in well-known phrase already 'manufactured articles.' We sometimes, for example, hear vague thinkers speak as if during the evolution of organic life animal instinct had been developed, *proprio motu*, into human reason ; blind giving rise to conscious purpose. But no such thing as blind or unconscious purpose is conceivable ; it is only another name for purposeless purpose, a plain contradiction in terms. Instinctive action, like the weaving of a spider, or the building of a bee, purposive action—that is to say, of whose purpose its immediate agent is apparently unconscious, must imply conscious purpose in the ground reality behind the immediate agent. Thus, if instinct ever even appears to pass up into reason, it can only be because it is already itself the product of reason. And the same thing is true of all analogous cases of what is called evolutionary progress."
And, once more, evolution " originates nothing, it invents nothing, it causes nothing. It is only a name for the gradual way in which God's

purposes are unfolded in the field of existence ; and the gradual way whereby in the field of knowledge they come to be recognized by man ; " and lastly, the very important thought, in view of what is said in the opening chapters of the present work : " The length of evolutionary process cannot affect the preliminary condition without which it could never have begun." [1] In the following pages the " ground reality," that is to say, the guiding of God Almighty, is assumed to be the real motive power by virtue of which the gradual growth, among very diverse peoples, of all that is included in the expression " Messianic Idea," became possible ; not only so, but it is also held that at the earliest dawn of man's understanding the germ, from which was later evolved what in their essence are the eternal truths of Messianism, was already implanted. To adapt Dr. Illingworth's words, the seed which we describe as potential Messianism is packed with that potentiality from the beginning of its existence.

By the phrase " The Evolution of the Messianic Idea " is therefore meant the method whereby the conception of a Saviour, overcoming all that is harmful to man and bringing about for man a state of peacefulness, became gradually more and more understood and apprehended by men.

[1] *The Doctrine of the Trinity*, chap. i.

THE EVOLUTION OF THE MESSIANIC IDEA

But secondly, there is the further danger that in studying Messianism on the comparative method one should be tempted to regard the subject in every presentation of it, including the specifically Christian, as nothing more than the history of a phase of thought; in a very interesting article Professor Mackintosh thus describes the attitude of a certain school of thought towards this subject: " There was a vague Messianic idea in the world, the argument runs; there was a kind of redemption-myth current in pious minds scattered over the Roman Empire in a hundred varied forms, and these impalpable, yearning dreams of salvation were deposited, like crystals in a super-saturated solution, on the idealized name of Jesus of Nazareth. It came to be believed that He had done and suffered all things expected of the Christ. You can explain what was thought of Him from the fermenting ideas of the time; Eastern Gnosticism and syncretistic Judaism will virtually cover the whole field. The conception of a divine Saviour who came down from heaven and returned thither is one whose intellectual antecedents we know exactly, and nothing could have been more natural than its appropriation by adoring believers, eager to deck the object of their faith with all possible names of honour." [1] Although disciples

[1] *The Expositor*, Sept., 1907, pp. 224 f.

ABSOLUTE TRUTH

of this school have undoubtedly a great deal which they are able with justification to urge in favour of their theory, they start upon the assumption, often tacit, that Jesus Christ was not what He claimed to be—God; and this is an assumption which does not seem justified when *all* the facts are taken into consideration. This is not the place to enter into the details of such facts, they are only referred to in order that the present writer may make his standpoint clear. But one consideration should be briefly mentioned; granted the existence of such a thing as Absolute Truth, which from its nature must have always existed, for it must of necessity be independent of Time, then the fact that among various peoples and at different times of the world's history scintillations of such Truth should have appeared to the profounder minds and have been utilized by these deeper thinkers, seems to be in the nature of things. If one takes, for example, the belief in God, the Creator, of whose existence no thinking man would, presumably, at this time of day decline to believe in, here is part of the Absolute Truth of the Universe; but this belief is not weakened because we know that in bygone ages men had quaint conceptions concerning the Deity; on the contrary, the conviction is justified that just because the absolute truth and reality of the existence of God was ever-present,

THE EVOLUTION OF THE MESSIANIC IDEA

therefore in the inexorable nature of things men could not help contemplating it; and if their ideas upon the subject were curious, that did not affect the reality of the underlying truth. Even at the present day we are forward to confess that not yet do we know even as we are known;[1] the truth of a thing is not affected by our partial realization of it. And as with the belief in God, the Creator, so with that in the Messiah, the " Anointed " or " Chosen " Saviour of the world;[2] the existence of conceptions concerning Him which were crass and materialistic among all kinds of peoples, ages and ages ago, is no proof that the underlying ideas which gave birth to them were not true in their essence. So far from the antecedents, on account of their inadequateness and incompleteness, being used for impugning the reality of the truth in its developed form, may one not be rather justified in recognizing elements of truth in the former on account of the proved truth of the latter? Because an acorn does not exhibit the trunk, root, branches and leaves of an oak, it is not therefore not potentially an oak; rather, just because we know the latter in its completeness, we are justified in seeing in the former, potentially, all that the latter contains. And therefore, although it is

---

[1] 1 Cor. xiii. 12.
[2] See Luke xxiii. 35; and cf. Enoch li. 3.

METHOD OF REVELATION

fully realized that this argument would not appeal to the school of thought referred to above—for this latter seems to regard the developed form of a truth as false because it sees no truth in its antecedents—we see in the numberless signs of Messianism from the earliest times onwards so many struggles in the attempt to articulate Eternal Truth ; an evolutionary process, but one wherein the " evolution " is rather that of the human mind in apprehending truth, than in the truth itself.

It has been said above that it is not possible for a believer to conceive of a time during which God's interest in His highest creation was not actively shown forth ; and therefore it must be the fact that untold millenniums ago, as soon as thought became articulate in man, the Spirit of God was working, and, as far as the very limited capacity of human beings permitted, revealing Himself in their hearts ; for it must have been in this self-revelation to man that the divine activity was displayed, though men knew it not.

To the question, How was the divine revelation to be received by man in this early stage ? very varying answers have been given ; two things concerning it may, however, be regarded as absolutely certain : firstly, that it must have been given in accordance with man's capacity for apprehension, and, secondly, that it must have been " in divers

THE EVOLUTION OF THE MESSIANIC IDEA

portions and in divers manners." [1] Now it is one of the main objects of the following pages to try and show that " Messianism "—the word being used, of course, in its widest sense—was, in its original essence, the outward expression of some elemental characteristics in man ; that it was, as already hinted above, originally one of those things which (like Religion itself, from which it is inseparable) was inevitably bound to assert itself—in a word, that the articulate expression of the underlying ideas which ultimately gave birth to the general term " Messianism," with all that it implies, lay in the nature of things. But when it is asked what *form* the outward expression of these elemental characteristics in man, whereby " Messianism " in its earliest stages was presented to the world, assumed, we approach a subject which can only be treated from a theoretical point of view ; and the theory here advocated is that the form which the outward expression of these elemental characteristics took was that which we call *Myth*. It will, however, be necessary, in order to show the justification of this theory, to touch very briefly upon the subject of the nature of myths.

The word " myth " is often applied to something in order to express the fact that it has no existence ; this is an inaccurate, or at any rate

[1] Heb. i. 1.

MEANING OF MYTH

an incomplete, use of the word, for it only takes into consideration part of that of which a myth, in the true sense of the word, consists. The myth, properly speaking, consists of two parts: an idea, and the way in which this idea is expressed; it is the latter which is too frequently taken to be the whole content of a myth, whereas this, in reality, stands to the underlying idea of the myth in the same relation as the husk does to the kernel. Man, in an early stage of civilization, requires his ideas to be presented pictorially—it would have been impossible for him to have imparted them otherwise; the picture, or more strictly speaking, the pictorial narrative, which enabled the idea to become articulate, would have lasted on long after man had reached the stage in which the idea could be apprehended without the medium of such pictorial narrative, and, in consequence, the relationship between the two was first obscured, and then often wholly lost sight of. It is, no doubt, in great measure, due to this divorce that the real nature of the myth is so often incompletely apprehended. The myth, being in its essence an *idea*, originated in the mind of man, and arose from the free play of his thoughts;[1] but the impulse which prompted this was a

[1] Wholly different therefore from the *legend*, which is a narrative based, in the last instance, upon some actual fact.

THE EVOLUTION OF THE MESSIANIC IDEA

divine one ; it was, according to the theory here advocated, the way in which the first beginnings of the knowledge of God came to man—inspiration in the most real sense of the word, though of a nature adapted to the limited capacity of apprehension of primitive man ; in a word, the mode of God's self-revelation to man at a time when, from the nature of the case, no other was possible. Myths, that is to say, so far from being, as was once generally believed, the work of the Devil, were at one time the normal means of divine revelation.

It should, however, be added that myth, in its earliest and simplest form, is a different thing altogether from Mythology, as that word is now used. Myth and Mythology are, under some circumstances, to be differentiated from each other much in the same way in which primitive and mediæval Christianity are ; not that the analogy holds good all through, far from it ; but just as the pure simplicity of Apostolic Christianity had in the Middle Ages become so permeated with and enveloped by all kinds of evil influences (even after allowing for all legitimate and necessary development) as to be scarcely recognizable, so the childlike and innocent character of primeval myths became, later on, so entangled and overlaid by poisonous growths, that their original purpose, of proclaiming eternal

MYTHS UTILIZED

truths to man, became gradually obscured, and finally obliterated. That they did originally proclaim divine messages to man must be granted if with the prophet of old we believe that God is " from everlasting " (Hab. i. 12) ; [1] and as the elemental characteristics of human nature, referred to above, were of divine creation, there cannot be anything incongruous in the thought that these were utilized for expressing certain myths which contained the germs of eternal truth.

[1] See the writer's pamphlet, *Religion a permanent need of Human Nature*, pp. 11-13 (1906).

PART I.

The Antecedents of the Messianic Idea.

PART I.

THE ANTECEDENTS OF THE MESSIANIC IDEA.

CHAPTER II.

THE EARLIEST FORMS OF MYTH DUE TO ELEMENTAL CHARACTERISTICS IN MAN.

SOME elemental characteristics in primitive man considered : (i) Superstitious fear, owing to animistic conceptions ; (ii) The sense of dependence on a higher power ; (iii) The desire to be happy—Primitive man, in giving articulate expression to these elemental characteristics, framed some of the earliest forms of myth.

THE dominant sensation in the spirit of early man was one which was akin to despair. The word is used as the *intensive* expression of a feeling which, in less outspoken form, was the normal mental state of man during the childhood of the human race. As far as can be gathered from the available *data*, fear and perplexity, together with a general sense of uneasiness, seem to have overshadowed and permeated the " Gemüth " of men while in the lower stages of civilization. Nor is it difficult to understand why this should have been the case. For, in the first place, to early man the daily strenuous

THE EVOLUTION OF THE MESSIANIC IDEA

struggle for existence must often have been grim and terrible ; no matter how favourable the natural conditions of his environment, there was always a difficulty in maintaining his existence. Uncertainty as to whether he would be able to find food was ever present ; this in itself was sufficient to give rise to a general spirit of discontent, born of incessant, harassing worry. To early man it was an unkind world. Added to this was the far more serious occasion for uneasiness and alarm owing to animistic conceptions. Apart from the belief that every stone, tree, river, etc., partook of life in a way which was not to be differentiated from human life—a fact which must have been the source of mysterious fear at every turn—there were the more tangible causes of dread which floods, storms, volcanoes and the like, presented, all, of course, due to the vindictive agency of unseen powers. " Man's impotency to resist the forces of Nature, and their terrible ability to injure him, would inspire a sense of terror, which in turn would give rise to the two-fold notion of omnipotence and malignity. The savage of the present day lives in perpetual fear of evil spirits ; and the superstitious dread which I and most others have suffered is inherited from our savage ancestry." [1] The mental process which led to

[1] Coke, *Tracks of a Rolling Stone*, p. 42 (1905).

ACTIVITY OF THE DEPARTED

this belief, is not altogether easy to fathom, but the subject has a bearing—indirect, it is true—upon that of the present investigation, and deserves, therefore, a passing notice. The development of every religious system presupposes a stage during which the cult of the departed was in vogue; that many natural phenomena were put down to the agency of the departed, and that thus belief in the existence of gods ultimately arose, has much which may be urged in its favour. Belief concerning the departed has, speaking generally, passed through two stages, not counting an earlier stage during which nothing definite was held as to their whereabouts, or as to their doings. At a very early period primitive man must have speculated upon the condition of his departed fellow-man. One thing there never seems—as far as the available *data* go to show—to have been any doubt about, namely a continuation of his existence after death; so that what early man had to satisfy himself about was concerning the whereabouts of the departed, and the nature of his activity. As regards his whereabouts, the first stage of belief seems to have been that he continued to live, invisibly, in the same surroundings as he did before death; the manner of such existence was probably, in the first instance, not thought of or inquired about, and would not have presented any difficulty, owing to the belief concerning a man's soul, a belief which was practically universal at one stage in the development of these speculations. The soul was an entity wholly distinct from the body, which it used as a temporary dwelling-place, and which it could leave, and sometimes did leave, at will. The individuality of the soul was regarded as something independent of the body ; at death it permanently left the body, but continued its activity on earth, sometimes to the detriment, sometimes, but less frequently, to the advantage of men.

It was a later stage of speculation when a definite locality was assigned, in the unseen world, to the souls of the departed. Here we are concerned with the earlier stage only, when the world was believed to be peopled with the invisible spirits of men who once lived there in the body, and whose activity was mostly inimical to human beings—an activity which was therefore the cause of manifold fear to the dwellers on earth.

It is not easy to decide what must have been the course of speculation on the part of primitive man concerning his animistic conceptions. If one tries to fathom his mental attitude towards his inanimate surroundings, one feels that his earliest thoughts about them must have been founded upon the analogy of the only thing that was within his experience, viz. himself ; as he was alive, there was, to him, no reason for denying life to anything else. His arguments were necessarily founded upon what was within his cognizance ; and all the world was mysterious to him as soon as he began to think about it, excepting himself ; *that* he could, or thought he could, understand ; therefore he argued from himself : " Because I am alive, so is that." And only too frequently when the sign, to him, of life in these things was manifested, it was such as to fill him with fear ; volcanoes, falling rocks, hurricanes, over-flowing rivers, etc., were so many signs of living wrath. And even when he had not experienced such occurrences himself, his fear would not be the less for being founded on hearsay.

So far, according to the view here advocated, primitive man imputed life to inanimate objects because he *naïvely* judged of them from the analogy of himself. He was still in the stage of only being capable of speculating upon what was visible. Sooner or later the subject referred to above, of man's invisible soul, must have arisen. The question of its whereabouts and activity after death must then have profoundly occupied his thoughts. It is a reasonable supposition to hold that he imputed to the activity of the departed what in times past had been regarded

THE EVOLUTION OF THE MESSIANIC IDEA

as due to the innate life of the objects of his surroundings. What before had been the irresponsible and insensate activity of mountain and river, was now believed to be due to the activity of departed souls. Fear was transferred, and at the same time intensified. One need not endorse the theory that fear was the origin of religion in saying that fear of what he conceived to be supernatural powers was a more or less constant sensation in early man. These beings of dreaded power, erratic and mostly vindictive, must have inspired man with terror for untold ages; and this vague and undefined fear caused by animistic beliefs, and later by the belief in the activity of the departed, must have become part of his natuie. " Through what vast ages man remained the victim of fear and unrest can be guessed at only by the relatively very recent period in his history during which reason has controlled and disciplined feeling. It has been truly said that 'nervous instability must have been a normal character of primitive man,' and it may be added that it remains a characteristic of the vast majority of mankind to this day. We have not altered so much as, taking too hasty glances over narrow seas, we are apt to think. In structure and inherited tendencies each of us is hundreds of thousands of years old, but the civilized

THE SENSE OF DEPENDENCE

part of us is recent. The influences of a few generations, acting from without, are superficial contrasted with the heritage of chiliads which explains our mental as well as our bodily rudimentary structures." [1]

But besides this pessimistic vein and this spirit of fearfulness which, there is every reason to believe, were so characteristic of early man, there was also an overpowering *sense of dependence*: this is, of course, a natural consequence of animistic conceptions. Whether the powers whereby early man conceived himself to be surrounded were regarded by him as supernatural or merely superhuman is immaterial in view of the fact that he believed himself to be dependent upon them for everything he required. The fact that this sense of dependence is characteristic of every form of religion, the lowest as well as the most spiritual, is sufficient proof that it is an element in man which is proper to his nature. What Dr. Otto says of man in the highest stage of culture hitherto reached, is in its degree true of early man: " There is the desire on the part of religion to bring ourselves and all creatures into the ' feeling of absolute dependence ' and as the belief in creation does, to subordinate ourselves

---

[1] Clodd, *Animism*, p. 46; cf. Jevons, *Introduction to the History of Religion* (3rd. ed.), *passim*, especially pp. 105, 233; Crawley, *The Tree of Life*, pp. 172 ff.

THE EVOLUTION OF THE MESSIANIC IDEA

and them to the Eternal Power that is not of the world, but is above the world." [1]

One other point needs to be touched upon for our present purpose here; the *desire to be happy* is ingrained in the heart of man; this is so self-evident that the bare mention of the fact is sufficient. It will, however, be obvious that this element in his nature must have very profoundly affected the mental development of early man; and it is upon this point that stress is laid now.

There are thus these elements—pessimism, with which is associated in the closest possible manner the sensation of fear; secondly, the sense of dependence; and thirdly, the desire for happiness—elements which to early man were constituent parts of his nature, and which he must, therefore, have begun to experience as soon as he was capable of taking cognizance of his surroundings. These, in proportion as man's mental development proceeded, must, up to a certain point, have gone on influencing his thought more and more.

It is not felt necessary to enter into detail here regarding these points; they are so amply illustrated in books on Anthropology and Folk-lore,

[1] *Naturalism and Religion* (Engl. Trans.), p. 41; cf. Jevons, *op. cit.*, p. 23; and for numerous examples of this sense of dependence, see Frazer, *The Golden Bough* (2nd ed.) *passim*.

THE CAUSES OF PRIMEVAL MYTHS

and are so obvious to every student of human nature, that they may be regarded as axiomatic. But if this be granted, it will follow that, as fundamental elements in human nature every department in the mental and spiritual evolution of man must have been profoundly affected by them. And this leads to the supposition that not only were the results of the play of his imagination on the part of early man—when he had reached that stage of mental development at which this became possible—coloured by these elements, which went to make up his mental equipment, but that they were the immediate cause of the earliest forms of primeval myth. To be sure, all early myths in their original form were, in great measure, suggested by visible environment, and the ætiological element must have very early entered into man's speculations; these, however, formed but the framework; the actual pictures were filled in and painted by something more deep-seated than that which only came through the material eye, or that which was prompted by mere curiosity; while these gave the form, it was the elemental part of human nature which invented the substance.

These cursory considerations are intended to hint at what the writer conceives to have been the origin, in their primeval form, of some world-wide myths, which (it is held) form the antecedents

THE EVOLUTION OF THE MESSIANIC IDEA

of the *Messianic Idea*. The starting-point of these will, in view of the main object of these pages, naturally be their Old Testament form. As the fact of the existence of these myths is, for the present purpose, of more importance than the reasons of their origin, it is not thought appropriate to pursue this latter subject beyond the mere mention of the points enumerated above, though various elements in the myths themselves will recall what has been said.

CHAPTER III.

FLOATING MYTH-MATERIAL WAS USED BY OLD TESTAMENT WRITERS AND ADAPTED TO HIGHER TEACHING.

For the present purpose only a restricted number of myths come into consideration—In the case of these single original forms are not to be postulated, since they are the expression of human characteristics all the world over—The three myths to be examined; those of (i) A primeval cruel monster who became identified with the watery element; (ii) A divine-human Hero who saved men from the monster, and brought them material blessings; (iii) A happy time long ago—A floating myth-material was utilized by some of the Old Testament writers, and adapted to more spiritual uses—In their *Hebrew* form these three myths may be designated: (i) The " Tehom-myth "; (ii) The " Jahwe-myth "; (iii) The " Paradise-myth."

These elemental characteristics in early man were, then, it is maintained, expressed by certain myths. But to avoid being misunderstood, it is necessary to lay stress on the following points. Firstly, one is very far from supposing that *all* early myths owe their origin to the desire to express in tangible form the innate feelings of man; there can be no shadow of doubt that many very early myths are merely ætiological in character. According to the theory here advocated, *some* myths were, in their origin, due to elemental human characteristics, therefore it would naturally only be to a *restricted number* of myths that the theory would apply; for when once the idea of myth had arisen, it would be used for other purposes than the original one, and there were hundreds of things ready to hand to supply the materials for such myths when once the " mythic concept " had come into existence. *It is, therefore, only to some myths that reference is here made*; though it is believed that these particular myths must, in their original form, have been among the very first that were conceived. Secondly, it is the thought in the *original form* of these myths that is essential for our present purpose, in the first instance; doubtless it is impossible to get at such original forms themselves as they must once have existed, for every myth has been so overlaid with extraneous matter, so modified through adaptation, and consequently so altered in appearance through the thousands of years of its history, that to recover it in its primitive simplicity is obviously out of the question. Nevertheless, in each case the early myth is the elaboration of an idea or feeling; underlying it is the conception to which its origin is due; it may, therefore, be possible to get at this underlying idea, this root-conception, in spite of the luxuriant growths that overshadow it. The attempt is, at all events, worth making; for if the root-conception can be laid bare, the *raison d'être* of the

FLOATING MYTH-MATERIAL

myth can at once be apprehended, and, for the present purpose, this is of cardinal importance.

But if, as is here maintained, there are some myths which are the result of speculations which elemental characteristics in primitive man gave birth to, then we shall not have to presuppose a *single* original for such myths ; the underlying idea or emotion will, in each case, cause the myth to be formulated in different, it may be many, centres ; so that much floating material would have been in existence for many ages before that stage of culture was reached in which such floating material could have been adapted to higher forms of belief. And here one must lay stress on the fact of the *paucity of ideas* among men in a low stage of civilization ; this cannot be too strongly insisted upon. For example, if the innate emotion of fear, nourished in the way indicated above, should have induced the belief in the existence of some cruel primeval power, there were not many ways open to primitive man, owing to the paucity of his ideas, of expressing in tangible form wherein this power existed ; there were not many ways open to him of presenting to himself what this power was, and what was its nature. In framing his ideas upon the subject, he *could* only start from his observations of his surroundings ; abstract thought must have been, as yet, impossible to him ; the cruel power must, according to his ideas, have presented itself to him in some visible form. And the outward things which his dim understanding could connect with this cruel power were very few in number ; the choice lay between dry land, water, and sky. But the terrors that existed on land could, to a large extent, be "understood"; and such things as earthquakes, volcanoes and landslips, were not of sufficiently frequent occurrence to induce him to connect a primeval cruel power with the dry land. The sky he probably did not originally think about, and, at any rate, he got very little harm from it, for thunder-storms and the like, while inspiring terror, could not necessarily, or very often, have damaged him. It was very different when he contemplated the sea, or large rivers ; here was something constantly in motion, something of fearful power, and which showed its power frequently ; something that would swallow up men and beasts. There can have been nothing which inspired men with so much terror, or which did them so much harm, as the element of water ; in the raging sea, in lakes, in overflowing rivers, in torrents of rain, and even in waterfalls, men found more to be afraid of than in anything else of their surroundings. It must, therefore, have been with this that they naturally associated any speculations which they had regarding a primeval cruel power. And if this is so, then there is no

THE ELEMENT OF WATER

difficulty in believing that speculations of a more or less similar character were entertained wherever men lived in the vicinity of rivers, lakes, or seas.[1]

It is worth recalling the fact that at an earlier period of the earth's history the total quantity of the element of water was far greater than at present. All authorities are agreed that man in an early form was present on the earth during the Pliocene period (end of Tertiary) ; therefore he must have existed through the Pleistocene period, which followed. But the early Pleistocene period was attended by a submergence of considerable areas; this is evidenced by the position of marine sands, gravels, shelly beaches, etc. ;[2] our human ancestors who lived through this had, for many ages, passed the most primitive stage. As it was, generally speaking, a necessity for early man to live near seas, lake-shores or river banks, he must have experienced during the disturbed Pleistocene periods constant catastrophes (caused, as he would believe, by the direct agency of the watery element) of the most appalling kinds; the tradition of these would be handed on. According to Huxley, man at this period was of a brutal type, short, powerful, hairy, with massive prognathous jaws, and small brain-pan ; while devoid of physical

[1] Cf. A. Clodd, *The Story of Primitive Man*, pp. 182–88 (1902).
[2] Windle, *Remains of the Prehistoric Period in England*, p. 3 (1904).

fear, he was superstitious in the highest degree.[1]
It is an acknowledged fact that the religious conceptions of man are influenced by his physical environment ; therefore one may feel justified in believing that the facts referred to above have played their part in influencing early man in the development of his conceptions.[2]

Or again, if, as is maintained, it is, generally speaking, an elemental characteristic in man to depend upon, and look for help to, those who are stronger than himself in times of need, then there would be forced upon him speculations as to what power it was that prevented the " primeval cruel power " from not being more in evidence than was actually the case. But more ; just as his innate emotion of fear expressed itself in framing the myth of the " primeval cruel power," associated with the sea, etc., so one is justified in supposing that he regarded the good things (such as they were) which he enjoyed as being due to a beneficent power of some sort ; his innate characteristic of dependence would suggest this. It would probably have been a later development which connected the " Bringer of blessings " with the

[1] Cf. Hutchinson, *Prehistoric Man*, p. 26 (1896). For these references I am indebted to Prof. A. S. Underwood, M.R.C.S.

[2] Cf. Lagrange, *Études sur les religions Sémitiques*, pp. 335–336 (1903).

THE DESIRE FOR HAPPINESS

beneficent power which curbed the fury of the primeval monster. At the same time, it is important to bear in mind the fact that the watery element which was identified with this primeval cruel power was still present; if men came to believe that it was not so powerful as of old, nevertheless its visible presence, and its still continued ravages, would tend to show that it was not yet entirely annihilated. This is a point which will come before us later on, and which will perhaps explain an element in some later forms of the myth which would otherwise appear difficult to account for. But again, in the case of this myth, there is no necessity to postulate one original form; the underlying idea was one which was common to man; therefore one would look for myths of a fundamentally similar character in widely separated centres.

And, once more, if the desire for happiness is an innate characteristic of man, then, sooner or later, the desire would crystallize into definite day-dreams; and in the nature of things men would communicate to each other their yearnings and aspirations, so that some fixed ideas on the subject would gradually be evolved; these, being handed on from generation to generation, would by degrees assume the shape of a regular tradition; and such a tradition would inevitably come to be regarded as the echo of something

THE EVOLUTION OF THE MESSIANIC IDEA

that did once upon a time actually happen; and men would yearn for the happy time that once existed long ago; and by degrees there would be formulated a definite hope that in time to come that happy time would once again be realized; and thus, finally, the hope would develop into a fixed expectation. And if this fixed expectation were brought into connexion with the "beneficent power" who had already curbed the "primeval cruel power," and who had brought manifold blessings, this would be a process of reasoning which would have been entirely natural. And therefore this, too, might well have originated among widely separated peoples, so that there would be no necessity to believe in a single original form of the resultant myth.

There may have been, and probably were, other myths which owed their origin to similar sources; but for our present purposes the three adumbrated above, which were the result, originally, it is believed, of speculations due to elemental characteristics in primitive man, are all that need be taken into consideration. They constituted a floating myth-material, it is held, for many ages among many races of men; and when the mental development of man had reached that stage in which religion, in the higher sense of the word, could be formulated, this floating material, as was natural, was utilized and

TRACES OF FLOATING MYTH-MATERIAL

adapted for the purposes of inculcating more exalted beliefs.

As our investigation is concerned primarily with the Old Testament, it is there that traces of the previously existing floating material must first be sought, together with the Old Testament forms into which the resultant myths have become crystallized. It is not intended to deal exhaustively here with these myths ; it will be sufficient to refer to the various standard works in which this is done ; but there are certain points in them, more especially in their biblical form, which must be brought out and laid stress upon, for they are important for dealing with the subject in hand. It will also be necessary to refer to some typical examples of each myth in different centres of its existence ; for the wide diffusion, in varying form, of each of these three myths is important as showing that the underlying idea in each case is such as is common to man. As already said, to postulate a single prototype in the case of every early myth seems to be unnecessary, if it gives expression to something that all men feel. Within a given area, no doubt, an original parent-myth has given birth to many daughter-myths, as for example in the Semitic area ; but to suppose that, for example, because a Saviour (Benefactor)-myth is found among the Algonquins of North America as well as among

Hebrews and Greeks, therefore all point to a common original, is quite unnecessary, if, as we have seen some reason to suppose, the root-idea in each form expresses something which is common to man. What Usener says in reference to myth-variation within a more restricted area—though he is, of course, referring to the variation of a single original myth—is, in principle, applicable in other directions : " It must not be supposed that the study of the comparison of myths can be restricted to their forms as found among different races. Every race which has been more richly developed, intellectually—above all the Greeks—possesses in the traditions of its clans and country districts—at times, even, in one and the same locality—a number of varying forms of one original myth. And not only are the same pictorial ideas presented in many different connexions ; for the more important a particular conception appeared to a people, the more certain was it at different times to have ramified into various directions and to have clothed itself in new forms."[1] Just as within a restricted area a given material in the shape of some ancient myth is utilized for evolving variations which differ very widely from the parent-myth, while a single underlying idea can be recognized in each variation, so within an unlimited area a given material

[1] *Die Sintflutsagen*, pp. 80–81.

FLOATING MYTH-MATERIAL

in the shape of some elemental characteristic in man is utilized for evolving (or, rather, in this case, forces to the birth) many myths which in different centres vary enormously, but which in each case clothes the identical underlying idea.

The three myths, then, referred to above formed a great mass of floating material which, according to the theory here advocated, was the common property of many races. This material had been handed down, it may have been, for untold generations; it formed the background of the religious systems of peoples differing greatly in racial characteristics, and widely separated geographically. Among those who had received this material were the ancestors of the Israelites; and from time immemorial their religious conceptions had been coloured by it. It is certain that the Israelites believed that what was recounted in these myths had actually occurred long ago; it was therefore sacred to them. When, in course of time, by means of gradual, subjective revelation, more spiritual beliefs permitted of a deeper apprehension of the nature and personality of God, it followed of necessity that the more primitive beliefs were subjected to modification. The essence of the earlier material was, nevertheless, regarded as containing truth, but truth which had been incorrectly, or at least inadequately, expressed. But since it embodied truths, one can

THE EVOLUTION OF THE MESSIANIC IDEA

understand why the Israelite prophets based much of their teaching upon it.

In their Hebrew form the myths which constituted this floating material may be designated: The "Tehom–myth," the "Jahwe-myth," and the "Paradise-myth." To guard against seeming to be irreverent in speaking of a "Jahwe-myth," it should be explained that what is meant is that the Israelite teachers took a pre-existing myth, and brought the name by which they knew God into connexion with it. It is not intended to imply that there was a mythic figure among the Israelites known as Jahwe.

These myths we now proceed to deal with.

CHAPTER IV.

THE " TEHOM-MYTH."

This myth embodies the belief of which the root-idea is the existence of a primeval cruel monster who was identified with the principle of " evil," *i.e.*, harmfulness—Its Hebrew form is spiritualized, though antique *traits* are still clearly discernible; it represents, therefore, an echo rather than the original voice.

THE " Tehom-myth " presents us with a belief in which the root-idea is the existence of a primeval monster who was the embodiment of the principle of evil, and who was inimical to God and man. This primeval monster is identified with the Ocean. In the Old Testament the myth appears in a highly spiritualized form; signs are, indeed, not wanting to show that in some of its earlier forms it must have been much richer in mythological content; but as we now have it, this is for the most part obliterated. Nevertheless, sufficient remains to illustrate the main points required for our present purpose. The fact cannot be too strongly emphasized that in the early narratives in *Genesis* we have a number of disjointed accounts of myths, legends, and traditions, sometimes obviously incomplete, which were gathered from different sources and put together at different times by different people; the material from

THE EVOLUTION OF THE MESSIANIC IDEA

which selections were made must have existed for many ages before they were utilized and adapted by the Hebrew religious leaders ; and in the course of its history within the Israelite literature, it has been differently manipulated, and modified according to requirement. " The Hebrew narratives, and the traditions from which our Book of *Genesis* was compiled, went back into ages infinitely more remote. It was natural for the Hebrew historian to preface his record of the origin of the chosen people with a record of the origin of all nations, the origin of the human race, and the origin of the universe. The materials for such a preface were to hand. He has placed them before us in their simplicity and beauty, making selections from his available resources, so as to narrate in succession the Hebrew stories of the cosmogony, the primeval patriarchs, the Deluge, and the formation of the races. The fact that we have in these eleven chapters a narrative compiled from two or more different sources is now so generally recognized, that there is no need here for any preliminary discussion upon the subject. But besides these larger and more easily recognized sources of information, the compiler obviously makes use of other materials of which the archaic character is evident both from the style and from the subject matter."[1] Gunkel,

[1] Ryle, *The Early Narratives of Genesis*, pp. 1, 2 (1892).

MYTH-MATERIAL IN *GENESIS*

also, pointedly remarks : " From all these and other similar facts it follows, in the first place, that these ancient traditions did not originally exist in their present connexion, but must in the first instance have existed independently in oral form. This conclusion has not hitherto been sufficiently taken into account by the critics. It is the custom, at the present time, to emphasize, in one or the other instance, that the two traditions are independent of each other, and the fact is not realized that there is nothing extraordinary about this, but that it is rather the normal state of affairs. In the case of each of the primeval traditions, that of Paradise, etc. . . . none of necessity presupposes the existence of another form, or points to another as a natural continuation. . . . From this it appears that as far as the study of sources ("Quellenkritik") is concerned, one must not suppose that the original sources formed a connected series, or anything approaching this ; on the contrary, even the original collections will have consisted in the main of a number of traditions which were only loosely connected." [1]

What is here said is, however, not to be restricted to the book of *Genesis* ; it is applicable to many passages in some other books of the Old Testament, for the great mass of floating mythic material was handed on from mouth to mouth

[1] *Genesis*, pp. 1, 2 ; cf. pp. xvii.-lv.

THE EVOLUTION OF THE MESSIANIC IDEA

during, at least, the whole of the pre-exilic period of Israelite history, and this was supplemented during and after the exile by further extra-Israelite elements. " We may be sure that they (i.e. the Jewish writers) were much more interested in reports of Babylonian myths, which might serve to revive the fading colours of older Israelitish myths, long since largely indebted, directly or indirectly, to the mythic traditions of Babylonia." [1]

It follows, therefore, that in its present form, the " Tehom-myth " (as well as the others to be considered) represents an echo rather than the original voice. Nevertheless, the underlying conceptions can with reasonable certainty be discerned, and this is, after all, that which is really required for our present purpose.

[1] Cheyne, *Traditions and Beliefs of Ancient Israel*, p. 2 (1907).

CHAPTER V.

THE TEHOM-MYTH AMONG THE HEBREWS.

EXAMINATION of Biblical passages: Gen. i. 2, ii. 4 ff.;
Amos ix. 3*b*; Isa. xxx. 7; Isa. xxvii. 1; Isa. li. 9, 10;
Ps. lxxiv. 12-15; Ps. lxxxix. 9-11; Job xxvi. 12, 13;
Job xl. 25-xli. 26. These passages are not exhaustive,
but are intended to serve as examples.

[LITERATURE: Dillmann, *Die Genesis*, pp. 1-162
(1886).—Ryle, *The Early Narratives of Genesis*, pp.
1-23 (1892).—Gunkel, *Chaos und Schöpfung in Urzeit
und Endzeit* (1895).—Usener, *Die Sintflutsagen* (1899).—
Gunkel, *Genesis übersetzt und erklärt*, pp. i-lxxi, 55-71,
92-140 (1901).—Schmidt, *Jona, eine Untersuchung
zur vergleichenden Religionsgeschichte* (1907).—Cheyne,
Traditions and Beliefs of Ancient Israel, pp. 1-154 (1907).]

Tehom existed at the beginning of all things, for obviously Genesis i. 1 is in the nature of a chapter-heading rather than part of the narrative. Genesis i. 2 says: *The earth was waste and void, and darkness was upon the face of Tehom* ; the parallel account [1] of the beginning of all things (ii. 4 ff.) makes no reference to *Tehom* ; this silence is significant, for it must have been due to some specific purpose ; a purpose which is not far to seek, if there was a desire to substitute an account of the origin of

[1] Questions regarding the dates of compilation of Old Testament sources are here immaterial, as we are only concerned with fundamental conceptions, and these find expression, paled it may be, in the latest as well as in the earliest sources.

THE EVOLUTION OF THE MESSIANIC IDEA

things more in accordance with a pure form of *Jahwe*-worship than the *Tehom*-myth permitted. But the brief echo contained in Genesis i. 1 is supplemented by a number of other references in the Old Testament; these have, for the most part, been gathered by Gunkel,[1] but the essential ones for our present purpose must be briefly studied here. In these passages the "*Tehom*-myth" has become so inextricably bound up with the "*Jahwe*-myth" that Chapter VIII. must be to a large extent anticipated here. At the same time, it should be added that while from man's very nature the antecedents of the "*Tehom*-myth" necessitated those of the "*Jahwe*-myth," it is held that in the dim past the two were in the first instance, quite distinct.

If what has been said above as to some of the earliest forms of myth being the expression of elemental characteristics in primitive man, is in any sense true, it will be granted that at such an early stage in the history of man's mental development he would have been incapable of embodying in myth more than one idea at a time. No doubt at a very early age the two myths were combined, especially as one was logically demanded by the other, but as each contains a distinct idea, and as each sought to give expression to a different idea, it seems certain that the two myths

[1] *Schöpfung und Chaos*, pp. 29–114.

must originally have been distinct. The conception of a cruel primeval monster was brought about by one elemental characteristic; the thought of a hero coming to combat this monster, and thus help men against its vindictiveness, is another idea; and if it is certain that the one idea preceded the other, it will also seem certain that the myth to which each gave birth must also, in the first instance, have been distinct. It is for this reason, that although they are combined, for the most part, in their Old Testament forms, they are nevertheless to be treated separately.

The most important passages for our present purpose are the following:

(*a*) **Amos ix. 3**: *And though they be hid from my sight in the bottom of the sea, there will I command the Serpent, and he shall bite them.* The point of interest here is that the abode of the Serpent is designated; it is in "the depths of the sea" (*qarqaʻ hayyām*), where he is to remain until his final destruction; he is therefore not regarded as annihilated; the significance of this will be referred to later on. Cheyne holds that the Serpent, or Dragon, was not originally "the watery mass of chaotic matter personified," but that, "like the *tanninim* ("serpents," "dragons") in Psalm lxxiv. 13, he was not the great water itself, but *upon* it; . . . we infer, then, that in the original myth a company of sea-monsters, with one at their head, were imagined to be on the great waters "[1]; but passages like the one before us, as well as those like Genesis xlix. 25 (*Tehom that coucheth beneath*), Deuteronomy xxxiii. 13, where the same words occur, and Isaiah xxvii. 1 (*The dragon that is in the sea*), do not support this inference. It is also of interest to notice here the Serpent's obedience to Jahwe; the subjugation of the sea-monster is, as frequently, referred to in a way which shows that it was a matter of common knowledge; this is one of the main arguments for the contention that the prophets make use of material which had for long existed as common property.

(*b*) **Isaiah xxx. 7**: *For Egypt helpeth in vain, therefore have I called her Rahab that sitteth still* (R.V.). In this passage the words: *Therefore have I called her Rahab that sitteth still* (*hēm shābeth*), cannot be correct; *hem shabeth* only requires to be treated as one word (*hammāshbāth*) to give perfect sense; it may then be translated: " Therefore I called her ' Rahab the conquered ' (lit. ' the silenced ').[2] The title applied to Egypt was very appropriate, for her impotence had been referred to in the context. But the point of importance here is that the prophet represents Jahwe as the speaker (cf. ver. 8),

[1] *Op. cit.* p. 5.
[2] Gunkel, *Chaos*, ... p. 39.

ISAIAH XXX. 7; XXVII. 1

just as in verses 1-5 it is implied that the discomfiture of Egypt is Jahwe's doing (cf. the way in which a later writer made use of this passage, see below under Isaiah li. 9-10). When, therefore, as the reason of Egypt's humiliation by Jahwe, she receives the name of " Rahab the conquered "— that the significance and meaning of the name are well understood is taken for granted by the prophet—there must be a reference to some occurrence which was analogous to this. As the name of Rahab is a synonym for *Tehom*, there is some justification for seeing in this passage an echo of some punishment which was inflicted upon *Tehom* by Jahwe. It will be noticed that the term " Rahab the conquered," or " silenced," does not necessarily imply that the monster was finally destroyed. With this passage compare Job ix. 13.

(c) **Isaiah xxvii. 1:** *In that day shall Jahwe punish with his terrible, mighty, and powerful sword Leviathan the coiling serpent, Leviathan the crooked serpent; yea, he will slay the dragon that is in the sea.* The identification between Leviathan, the Serpent, and the Dragon that is in the Sea, is distinctly brought out in this passage. Moreover, Jahwe's conflict with the sea-monster also finds its place here. What is, however, particularly noteworthy is the fact that the whole action is placed in the future, " In that day " (cf.

THE EVOLUTION OF THE MESSIANIC IDEA

Ps. lxxiv. 14, referred to below); this is here for the first time definitely stated. This is therefore a new element, and it shows the significance of the fact, already noticed, that the sea-monster is nowhere said to have been finally destroyed; he is "silenced" (Isa. xxx. 7), "humbled" (Ps. lxxxix. 11), and, as in this passage, so in Psalm lxxiv. 14, his final destruction is yet to come; that is to say, he is still in existence, and apparently capable of doing harm (Amos ix. 3). The mythic element in this passage is emphasized by the mention of Jahwe's "sword"; the epithets applied to it seem to mark it out as something very special. The terms in which Leviathan is described are also noteworthy. Both the sword of Jahwe and Leviathan are spoken of without any explanatory comment, giving therefore again the impression that the reference was well understood, or in other words, that the prophet was utilizing material already existent.

(d) In **Isaiah li. 9–10,** *Tehom*,[1] or as he is called in this passage, *Tehom Rabbah*, receives also the name *Rahab*, a word which appears to come from the Assyrian *ra'âbu* (cf. *Oxford Hebrew Lexicon*, s.v.), and contains the root-ideas of "pride" and "restlessness." In this passage, too, "the waters of Tehom Rabbah" and the

[1] *Tehom* (Tiamat) is represented as of the male sex as well as the female, though the latter is more original.

ISAIAH LI. 9-10

" Sea " (*Yām*) are likewise identified ; and *Tehom* and *Tannîn*, " the Dragon," are evidently not to be differentiated. It is worth noting that in this passage the Septuagint omits 9*b* altogether, as it appeared to be practically repeated in 10*a* ; and instead of " Jahwe," in verse 9, the Septuagint reads " Jerusalem," perhaps regarding the mention of God's name in connexion with the myth as unfitting. But the salient point here is that it is clear from these verses that *Tehom* is known by the names *Rahab*, and *Tannîn*, and is identified with *Yām*, the " Sea " ; or, at all events, the Sea is personified as *Tehom*. But it appears, further, that *Tehom* must also be identified with *Hanaḥash*, " the Serpent " ; this is plainly implied in Amos ix. 3 : *And though they be hid from my sight in the bottom of the Sea, thence will I command the Serpent and he shall bite them.* The Serpent, again, is the same as Leviathan ; this comes out distinctly in Isaiah xxvii. 1 : *In that day Jahwe . . . shall punish Leviathan the gliding serpent*, etc., this passage shows the identity between Leviathan and the Dragon (*Tannîn*) ; see further Ezekiel xxix. 3 ; xxxii. 2 ; Job. xxvi. 12–13 ; Psalm lxxiv. 13–16.

To seek to catch the echoes which are sounded in these various Old Testament passages of the *Tehom*-myth, it is essential that the identity between *Tehom* and Rahab, Leviathan, the

Dragon, the Serpent, and the Sea should be recognized. In earlier forms of the myth it is probable that the sea-monster only appeared under one name; but the fact that so many have come to be applied to him suggests the existence of differing versions of the myth which had by degrees become incorporated into the body of floating material which the prophets made use of. The whole of this passage, Isaiah li. 9-10, deserves to be quoted on account of its important bearing on the subject in hand:

> *Rouse thee, rouse thee, put on thy strength,*
> *Arm of Jahwe;*
> *Rouse thee as in days of old, as in ages long since past;*
> *Art not thou that which " clave in pieces "* [1]
> *Rahab, that pierced the Dragon?*
> *Art not thou that which dried up the Sea, the waters of Tehom Rabbah?*
> *That made the depths of the Sea a way for the redeemed to pass through?*

Nothing could be clearer here than that a belief was current among the exiles that in the distant past Jahwe had fought against and overcome Rahab—the Dragon or Tehom Rabbah,

---

[1] The Hebrew rendering, *hamaḥāṣebeth*, comes from a root which usually has the sense of " to hew out," but might quite possibly be used in the way rendered above; a suggested alternative would be to read *hamᵉḥaṣeṣeth*, from the root meaning " to cleave."

PSALM LXXIV. 12-15

and that this victory was regarded as evidence of Jahwe's power to overcome all the difficulties that stood in the way of the exiles' return. In this passage, too, Jahwe's victory in the past is evidently assumed to be a well-known fact.[1] Nor does it appear that a figurative sense is intended, both on account of the employment of such words as *ḥāṣab*,[2] *hillēl*[3] and *ḥārath*,[4] and on account of the last clause, which especially refers to an historical fact (cf. Isaiah xliii. 16-19).

(e) **Psalm lxxiv. 12-15:**

> God is my king from of old,
> Working salvation in the midst of the earth;
> Thou didst split in twain the Sea in Thy strength;
> Thou didst break in pieces the heads of the dragons in the waters.
> Thou didst smash the heads of Leviathan;
> Thou wilt give him (*tittnennu*) for food—for food (read *lehem* for *leʿām*) to the "demons of the desert";[5]
> Thou didst cleave fountain and flood;
> Thou didst dry up ancient rivers.

[1] It is significant that this conflict is not referred to in the Genesis account, unless Genesis i. 9 is a pale allusion to it.

[2] "To cleave."   [3] "To pierce."   [4] "To dry up."

[5] In justification of this rendering of עִיִּים, see the writer's article, *The Demonology of the Old Testament illustrated from the Prophetical Writings*, in the *Expositor* (June, 1907), p. 529. Another suggested reading is *leʿām ṣiyyim*; in either case the meaning is "the denizens of the waste."

THE EVOLUTION OF THE MESSIANIC IDEA

We should expect " Jahwe " instead of *'Elohīm* in verse 12—the Septuagint (B*) has simply " Our King," though the MSS. B⁽ᵃᵇ⁾ אRT insert " God " before " King "; the psalm is wanting in Cod. Alexandrinus; the absence of אתה (" Thou ") which is the opening word of each of the other clauses, suggests a corruption in the text.

The same notes which are sounded in the preceding passages are heard here again. The reference is to something that happened long ago; God (Jahwe) overcame a great monster, who is the Sea personified, and who is also called Leviathan; he is not finally killed—it is significant that *tittnennu* (" thou wilt give him ") is the only verb not in the preterite; this accords with what has already been noticed; but he is at some future time to be devoured by demons. An echo of this tradition of the end of Leviathan is preserved in the Talmud (*Baba Bathra*, 74a), where it is said that in the times of the Messiah the *Ḥebārīm* (the " saints ") are to feast upon Leviathan (cf. Ezek. xxix. 5; xxxii. 4-6). The story is in this passage again assumed to be well known. A new feature, however, appears here, for Leviathan is accompanied by a brood of dragons (*Tannīnīm*), and he himself is represented as a many-headed monster; these seem to be later developments; the idea of Leviathan being the chief of an army of

PSALM LXXXIX. 9-11

dragons has perhaps not been without influence in the further stages of the history of the myth.

(f) **Psalm lxxxix. 9-11 (8-10):**

Jahwe, God of hosts, who is like unto thee, mighty Jah?

And thy faithfulness is round about thee.

Thou rulest the Sea when she rises up, thou stillest her waves when they roar (cf. the Septuagint);

Thou hast humbled (cf. the Septuagint) *Rahab, as one that is dishonoured* (cf. Ezek. xxi. 30);

With thy mighty arm (cf. v. 13) *hast thou scattered thine enemies.*[1]

The points of importance in this passage, from the point of view of the present discussion, are: firstly, that what is described is represented as having happened in the past;[2] but it is particularly interesting to notice that in spite of Jahwe's victory, His power has still to be exercised upon the enemy; although the humbling of Rahab and the scattering of the enemies has been

[1] On this passage cf. Gunkel, *op. cit.*, p. 33 (note).

[2] There is an obvious reference to the Creation in verse 12 (13 in the Hebr.) of the Psalm.

accomplished, nevertheless the Sea still rises up at times, and her waves roar, so that Jahwe has to exhibit His supremacy whenever this happens. Here, therefore, we have once more the fact brought out that the sea-monster has not yet been finally destroyed. Secondly, Rahab and the Sea are identified; and thirdly, the mention of the conflict is brought in incidentally, as being a thing of common knowledge. With the whole passage cf. Job ix. 13; xxvi. 12; the mention of Jahwe's "Arm" recalls Isaiah li. 9, it is perhaps to be connected with His mythic sword, already referred to, which is held by this "Arm."

(g) **Job xxvi. 12–13:** *With his might did he still the Sea* (cf. the Septuagint, Syro-Hexaplar and the Syriac Versions); *and with his skill* (lit. "understanding") *did he cleave in pieces (māḥaṣ, cf. Isa. li. 10) Rahab.*

Heaven's bolts were terrified at him (cf. the Septuagint)

He hath dishonoured with his hand the coiling Serpent (cf. Is. xxvii. 1).

The now familiar *data* about Jahwe's conflict are again in evidence here; Rahab is identified with the Sea, and with the "coiling Serpent," who is dishonoured, but not destroyed finally.

JOB XXVI. 12-13; XLI. 1-34

The mention of the terror of " Heaven's bolts " is a new feature (see below), showing, probably, further development of the myth, though it must be greatly older than the book of Job. The story is again referred to as well known.

(*h*) Finally, there is the long passage Job xl. 25–xli. 26, (xli. 1–34, E.V.), with its description of the monster of the deep, which is full of points of subsidiary interest and importance ; here it is only necessary to point out that Leviathan is throughout regarded as still existing, see especially xli. 2 (xli. 10. E.V.) ; no man can withstand him, but only Jahwe ; he is spoken of as a monster about whom everyone knows.

These passages, which could easily be supplemented, are sufficient for our purpose. The points to be emphasized in them are the following : *Tehom*, identified with the watery chaos which existed before the creation of the world, was a great primeval sea-monster ; there was a conflict between *Tehom* and Jahwe, in which the former was defeated, but not finally destroyed ; *Tehom* was also inimical to men ; there was an essential identity between *Tehom*, Leviathan, Rahab, the Serpent, and the Dragon ; and the Sea, which was her abode, is also sometimes identified with her ; the myth was clearly well known, and formed part of a large mass of myth-material which had been handed down for ages. At the foundation of all stands the figure of *Tehom*, the primeval cruel sea-monster.[1]

[1] The fact is not forgotten that there also exists in the Old Testament an entirely different conception regarding the element of water, according to which the watery mass, in so far as it moistens and fertilizes the parched ground, is a beneficent agency. But this fact is, of course, concerned with an entirely different set of ideas from those with which we are here dealing, and belongs to very much later times.

In some sense analogous to this are the opposite conceptions regarding the Sun, which is beneficent in so far as it ripens, etc., (e.g. Deut. xxxiii. 14), but harmful in that it " smites " with its heat, etc. (e.g. Is. xlix. 10.)

CHAPTER VI.

THE TEHOM-MYTH AMONG OTHER PEOPLES.

THE underlying idea of the " Tehom-myth " among the Hebrews is paralleled by other forms of this myth among many peoples ; this justifies the inference that in the Old Testament we have but one of the many expressions of a root-conception which is common to man—Examples of other forms of the " Tehom-myth " : Chaldæan, Phœnician, Egyptian, Zoroastrian, Greek, Algonquin, Iroquois, South American, Mexican, African, Peruvian—This list is far from being exhaustive.

[LITERATURE : Schoolcraft, *The Myth of Hiawatha* (1839).—Waitz, *Anthropologie der Naturvölker*, vol. vi. (1859 . . .).—J. Darmesteter, *Ormazd et Ahriman, leurs origines et leur histoire* (1877).—Baudissin *Studien* . . . I., pp. 11–46 (1878).—F. Lenormant, *Les origines de l'histoire d'après la Bible et les traditions des peuples orientaux* (2nd ed.) I., pp. 533–553 (1880).—West, *Pahlavi Texts*, part I., vol. v. of " Sacred Books of the East " series, edited by Max Müller (1880).—Bancroft, *History of the Pacific States of North America*, vol. iii. (1882 . . . .).—Brugsch, *Religion und Mythologie der alten Aegypter*, pp. 100–183 (1888).—Schoolcraft, *The Indian Tribes of the United States* (1891).—Brinton, *The Myths of the New World* (3rd. ed.) (1896). —Lang, *Myth, Ritual and Religion* (1901).—Pinches, *The Old Testament in the Light of the Historical Records of Assyria and Babylonia*, pp. 1–117 (1902).—Böklen, *Die Verwandschaft der jüdisch-christlichen mit der Parsischen Eschatologie* (1902).—Jeremias, *Das alte Testament im Lichte des alten Orients*, pp. 1–145 (1904).—Breysig, *Die Entstehung des Gottesgedankens und der Heilbringer* (1905).]

IT will be necessary, next, to show that, in its essence, the underlying idea of the " Tehom-myth " was not the exclusive possession of the

Hebrews. When it is found that in the Old Testament form of the myth there are certain elements which may be paralleled by other forms of the myth which are known to exist among many other peoples, there is some justification for the inference that in the Old Testament we have but one of the many expressions of a root-idea which was, in the first instance, common to man ; and thus the theory of a single original form of the myth will, on account of the widely separated areas in which the same root-idea finds expression, be excluded.

In referring to these other forms (which will be dealt with in the briefest possible manner), one turns naturally, first of all, to those of the Chaldæans, because between these and the Old Testament form there are many marks of affinity ; so much so, that, in this case, independent originals are not necessarily to be assumed ; here we have an instance, referred to above, of varying forms of one original occurring within a particular area, i.e., the Semitic.

In the *Chaldæan* accounts of what must here be called the *Tiamat*-myth, as in that of the Old Testament, there is the intermixture of two myths, originally distinct (cf. what was said above on this point). The root-ideas, which are common to the two accounts, are all that it will be necessary to point to here, leaving aside the

THE CHALDÆAN TIAMAT-MYTH

wealth of subsidiary detail with which the Chaldæan accounts abound.

Before the creation of the world Apsu (the Ocean) and Tiamat alone existed ; in the account given by Berossus, darkness and water were the only things in existence ; but a brood of monsters came into being, over which Tamte (=Tiamat, the Greek *Thalassa*) ruled. When the gods come into existence, warfare breaks out between them and Tiamat, Apsu and the brood of monsters. The champions on either side are Marduk (Bel =*Baal* according to Berossus) and Tiamat ; the arms of the former are the bow and arrows, sword, thunderbolt and net. Marduk is victorious; with his sword he cleaves Tiamat in two halves ; one half he places above, " a covering for the heavens," before which he draws a bolt, and places guards, charging them not to let her waters out ; the other half is placed below.

Comparing these main points with the Old Testament *data*, we have to note the following : The primeval watery monster that existed before all things, and darkness is associated with it (cf. Gen. i. 1) ; Tiamat's brood (cf. Ps. lxxiv. 13 ; lxxxix. 10-11) ; the conflict between Tiamat and Marduk, in which the latter is victorious (cf. Isa. xxx. 7 ; li. 9-10 ; Ps. lxxiv. 12-15 ; lxxxix. 9-11 ; Job xxvi. 12-13) ; with the sword of Marduk (compare Isa. xxvii. 1) Tiamat is cloven in twain (cf. Isa. li. 9-10); striking, too, is the fact that a bolt is drawn before the half which is placed above (cf. the Septuagint of Job xxvi. 13, *Heaven's bolts were terrified at him*) [1]; this suggests that in spite of defeat Tiamat was still capable of harm and had to be imprisoned; this, as we have seen, is a feature in almost all the Old Testament passages considered above.

In the very meagre remains which we have of a *Phœnician* cosmogony there is, nevertheless, enough to show a distinct relationship with the Babylonian and Old Testament narratives. The primeval watery monster again figures; her name, "Baau," interpreted to mean "Night," is sufficient indication of such relationship; while the mention of her spouse, Colpias ("The Wind, or Air, which is on every side"), given as the name of the Wind (*ruaḥ*), suggests an originally intimate connexion with what underlies Genesis i. 2: *And the earth was waste and void (Bohu), and darkness was upon the face of Tehom, and the Spirit (or Wind, ruaḥ) of God brooded upon the face of the waters.*

[1] Jeremias says that this bolt (Bab. *parku*) = the Zodiac; this would account for the plural "bolts" in the Septuagint rendering. He goes on to refer to *raqi'a*, (the "firmament") "which separates the upper waters from the lower," and to *ḥōq* ("boundary"), Ps. cxlviii. 4, which is fixed in order that the upper waters may not overstep their bounds. According to Genesis vii. 11, "the 'bolt' is taken away, and the upper and lower waters flow together" (*op. cit.* p. 55, cf. p. 78).

THE PHŒNICIAN ACCOUNT

In one of the Phœnician accounts it is these two who give birth to the Dragon; while, according to another, Adam and Eve are their offspring. Thus Sanchoniathon says: "Then were born of Colpia, the 'Wind,' and of his spouse 'Baau' (which is interpreted *nukta*, that is 'night,' by the Greeks) 'Aeon' and 'Primogenitus,' mortals both . . ."[1] On the other hand, Damascius; (*De prim. princip.*, 123) relates of the cosmogony of Hieronymus and Hellanicos,[2] according to Lenormant: "In the beginning there was water and moist soil which, in joining together, made the earth. Thus, as the primeval origin of things water and the earth are presupposed, water as representing the principle of division, of dissolution, the earth that of attraction and of cohesion; but the original source which existed before each of these is not mentioned. . . . A third principle is born of the union of the two that are called Water (the male) and the Earth (the female); it has the form of a dragon which has two heads joined together, those namely of a bull and of a lion. . . ."[3] It is easy to see that we have here very faint reminiscences; the contradictory nature of the

[1] Orelli, *Phœnicum Theologia ex Sanchoniathone; ex Eusebii "Praep. Evangel."* I. x. p. 15 (1826) Baudissin *op. cit.* I. chap. i.

[2] Cf. Josephus, *Ant.* I. iii. 9, who refers to the "Phœnicica" composed by Hieronymus the Egyptian and Hellanicos.

[3] *Op. cit.* pp. 533 ff.

tradition shows that only the underlying idea is to be relied upon, namely, that, as in the Babylonian and Biblical, there existed before all else a watery monster, who represented the principle of evil. No reference seems to be made anywhere in Phœnician tradition to a conflict with the monster—no importance can be attached to this silence, owing to the fragmentary character of the evidence, otherwise it would be interesting to have a form of the "*Tehom*"-myth unconnected with any form of the "*Jahwe*"-myth. Originally, as the present writer believes, the two were quite distinct, and they became connected—just as, in its turn, the "Paradise"-myth was later on added to the cycle—because the underlying ideas to which they were primarily due formed a logical sequence; this is referred to below.

Turning next to take a glance at *Egyptian* beliefs concerning this subject, one is naturally predisposed, owing to the large amount of intercommunication between Egypt,[1] Syria, and Babylonia in ancient times, to look for signs of mutual influence; and such signs certainly do exist. Though, in detail, Egyptian cosmogonical conceptions show many marks of individuality, yet in fundamentals agreement with the systems already referred to is clearly to be discerned. It

[1] Cf. Völter, *Aegypten und die Bibel* (3rd ed.), pp. 1, 2 (1907).

THE EGYPTIAN ACCOUNT

is probable that the original Semitic form of the myth lies at the bottom of the Egyptian accounts, and that, unlike some other forms to be considered, Egypt cannot lay claim to an independent origin. According to Brugsch, quoting from the monuments:

" In the beginning there was neither Heaven nor Earth. Enveloped in thick darkness the boundless primeval Deep (called ' Nun ' by the Egyptians) filled the ' All ' (Universe) ; this primeval deep secreted in its depth the male and female germs (or ' the beginnings ') of the future world ;[1] the Divine primeval Spirit, inseparable from the original matter of the primeval Deep, experienced the desire of creative activity, and his word called the world into being—the world, the appearance and manifold forms of which had beforehand been mirrored in his eye . . . .The first act of Creation began with the formation of an Egg from the primeval Deep, out of which Daylight (*Rä*), the immediate cause of life in the domain of the terrestrial sphere, came forth."[2] This passage offers a curious mixture of *naïveté* and somewhat advanced thought ; in its essence,

[1] Cf. (in a different connexion) in Zoroastrian belief, the seed of Zoroaster in the lake Kansu ; in time to come a maiden is to bathe in this lake, and conceive by the seed of Zoroaster ; she is then to give birth to the Shoshyans (cf. below).

[2] *Op. cit.*, p. 101.

however, it is only another way of saying : *The earth was waste and void ; and darkness was upon the face of the deep ; and the spirit of God brooded upon the face of the waters. And God said, Let there be light, and there was light.* The idea of the egg is an exceedingly antique *trait*, which is also presupposed in the Biblical account because of the word " brooded."[1] It will be noted that we have here only the mention of " a boundless primeval Deep," in connexion with which there are the psychologically contradictory thoughts of " Darkness " and " the Divine primeval Spirit." It is difficult to resist the conclusion that the original form of the myth has been wrested in the interests of later theological speculations ; it was necessary that *Rä*, " the immediate cause of life in the domain of the terrestrial sphere," should be represented as, at all events potentially, existent from all time, therefore he is spoken of as essentially part of the " Primeval Deep." Somewhat parallel to this is the Biblical (P) account, which prefaces the Creation story with : *In the beginning God created the Heaven and the Earth* ; while in the older form (J) these (see further below), are in existence before the divine creative action commences. In the Egyptian form, therefore, the " Darkness " is not treated as representing the principle of evil,

[1] Cf. the same idea in Manu i. 5 ff., and see Cheyne, *op. cit.* p. 9.

THE EGYPTIAN ACCOUNT

and therefore the primeval watery mass is not the enemy of gods and (later) of men. Quite in accordance with this, therefore, is the thought in another inscription (on the walls of the temple of Ombos) : " Sebek-rā (i.e. the Sun-Crocodile) who comes forth out of the primeval waters . . . the first of all the gods . . . the glorious figure of the crocodile who comes forth from the holy primeval waters, which exist from the beginning, of which all things are that exist." [1] But the idea of some great conflict, such as appears in the Biblical and Babylonian accounts, is not wholly absent, and though it is not parallel to these in its present form, it is worth referring to, as it may be an echo of an early myth which, like others, has gone through a process of adaptation. We quote Brugsch once more : ". . . In a representation on the walls of a sanctuary dedicated to the Theban Thot, in the Temple-group of Medinet-Abu, the same four pairs of gods appeared with their usual names : Nun-Amon, Nunet-Ament, Kekui-Kekuit, (Nen)-Nenet. The last-named goddess has, besides her ordinary name, the significant addition : *Hemset*, that is, ' The Sitting one,' or ' The Resting one,' to which the following words are added : ' The Snake who measured the world, and who in the beginning bore the god Cheper, the great Deep.' " [2] While the Serpent

---

[1] Brugsch, *op. cit.* p. 105.   [2] *Ibid.* pp. 143-144.

THE EVOLUTION OF THE MESSIANIC IDEA

here is identified with the primeval waters, and his *rôle* is so different from that which he occupies in the other systems mentioned, nevertheless the belief of a serpent in primeval times fighting against the God of Light appears in an inscription on a tomb in Qurna, which runs: " The Snake (Dragon) Apophis, the adversary of Rā." Apophis is, no doubt, conceived of as belonging to quite a different order from the Serpent, which gave birth to the god Cheper; but the question is whether the early myth has not been so manipulated and altered as to leave only traces, and these distorted, behind. Such a trace may perhaps, further, be discerned in the *Book of the Dead*, in the 17th chapter of which reference is made to a conflict between the Sun-Cat (i.e. Rā [1]) and his enemy; the god Tum speaks, according to Brugsch's translation, as follows: " I am the great Cat, beside whom Ashd-Baum stretched himself in (the celestial zone of) On, in that night of combat and of the refuge of the enemy, and on that day on which the adversaries of the All-Lord (Neb-ert'er) were destroyed. What does this signify? That great Cat was Rā himself...." [2] Once more, in another inscription there is a mention

[1] On a tomb in Qurna there is an inscription which runs: " The Cat into which the God Rā changed himself " (Brugsch).

[2] *Ibid.* p. 307.

THE ZOROASTRIAN ACCOUNT

of Hathor-Isis, who also has the local name of Ad, Adit, " She who wounds " ; she appears also as the cow of the primeval waters Uehit-ueret, who, in crossing the waters of Nun, protected her son Horus between her horns. In the same text, Hathor, as At or Ad, appears in the form of the cat who wounded the snake or dragon, Apophis.[1] The Dragon is, however, only wounded, not finally destroyed.

These references are, it is true, very indefinite ; but it seems possible to discern in them some faint echoes of an ancient myth, according to which there existed before all things a primeval watery mass ; and that a conflict took place long ago between the Sun-god Rā and a great dragon. These two points are, however, of prime importance, inasmuch as they form the kernel of the world-wide myth which we are considering.

In the *Zoroastrian* cosmogony there is one point of striking resemblance with the Egyptian, in that the evil principle Angra-Mainyu (of which Aharman is a corruption) did not precede Aûharmazd in existence [2]; this, one cannot help thinking, is due to the same cause that made Rā potentially existent in the primeval watery chaos. As we have seen, in the Biblical (J) account the heaven and the earth, and therefore of course

[1] Brugsch, *op. cit.* p. 306.
[2] *Bundahish* 1. 9.

THE EVOLUTION OF THE MESSIANIC IDEA

Tehom, are presupposed to be there before Jahwe; in the Chaldean account Tiamat is in existence before Marduk is mentioned; so, too, in the Phœnician account *Baau* appears as primeval. This is as one would expect; for the advanced thought of the Egyptian and Zoroastrian cosmogonies would necessitate a greater toning down of the original tradition, just as is found in the later Biblical (P) account. In its essence, however, the Zoroastrian form of the myth is analogous to the others referred to. The principle of evil, personified in Angra-Mainyu, is distinctly brought into connexion with the primeval watery mass; there is a great conflict between this " evil spirit who causes adversity " and the Lord of Light; but the evil spirit is not finally destroyed until the end of the world.[1] " Desirous of destroying, and because of his malicious nature, he rushed in to destroy that light of Aûharmazd unassailed by fiends; and he saw its bravery and glory were greater than his own; so he fled back to the gloomy darkness, and formed many demons and fiends; and the creatures of the destroyer arose for violence." [2] Elsewhere we read of Angra-Mainyu coming on to " the water which was arranged below the earth." [3] There is another

[1] See *Bund.* i. 20–22; xxxiv. 1; Darmesteter, *op. cit.* pp. 92 ff.
[2] *Bund.* i. 10; cf. *Zad-Sparam* i. 1–11.
[3] *Bund.* iii. 13; cf. *Zad-Sparam* ii. 3.

HESIOD'S ACCOUNT

account of the conflict in *Zad-Sparam* i. 5, which differs a little from the *Bundahish* account; according to this, the spirits of the waters, besides others, come to the assistance of Angra-Mainyu in his struggle with Aûharmazd. It will, therefore, be seen that, with the exception referred to above, the Zoroastrian cosmogony strikes some of the familiar notes.[1]

Brief mention may also be made of Hesiod's reference to the primeval watery mass, in his *Theog.* ll. 116–119[2]: "Verily Chaos was created first of all, and then broad-bosomed Earth, ever the safe seat of all the Immortals, who dwell on the peaks of snowy Olympus, and dark Tartarus in the recesses of the spacious Earth."

It is important to notice that here, as in most of the accounts dealt with, chaos is in existence before the gods.

Finally, it is worth noting that among the myths of many living races in a low stage of civilization, we come across distinct references to this primeval watery mass; it is by no means always personified, nor does it always appear as necessarily cruel or malignant; nevertheless there are reasons for thinking that between these and the forms of myth already spoken of there exists

---

[1] Cf. Böklen, *op. cit.* pp. 125–130.
[2] *Die Hesiodische Theogonie mit Prolegomena* (ed. Flach. 1873).

at bottom a community of ideas. To take but a few examples. The *Algonquins* of North America say that in the beginning a watery mass covered the whole of the earth, so that there was nowhere where the animals—who alone existed at that time—could dwell. In the quaint story of how Michabo, the Great Hare, by sending various animals, first the beaver, then the otter, and at last the musk-rat, to the bottom of the sea to bring up a morsel of soil, in order to make the earth out of it ; and of how Michabo increased this morsel of soil to the size of the earth by running up and down on it [1]—in this story we have another form of the ancient myth of the primeval watery mass which had to be overcome. Making due allowance for the savage way of putting things, it is clear that the underlying idea here is that the primeval flood had to be subdued, and that a hero, in the shape of Michabo, came forth and so far conquered the Ocean and drove it back, that room was made for the earth, upon which animals and men could then live ; the running up and down upon the patch of soil, and thus gradually increasing it by encroaching more and more upon the watery surface, represents what in other forms of the myth is the conflict between the rival powers. It is, therefore, not incorrect to

[1] The different accounts vary somewhat in detail.

OTHER ACCOUNTS

say that in the Algonquin myth the watery mass is regarded as inimical.

Connected originally with the Algonquin myth is that of the *Iroquois*[1]; here, too, a primeval watery mass existed before all things; over it (though how it came to be is not stated) were the heavens, from which Ataentsic "the sky-woman" fell; she fell into the water, but saved herself on the back of a tortoise; she then proceeded to make the earth out of a morsel of soil brought to her by a frog, or beaver, from the bottom of the sea.

According to the *Popol Vuh*, the holy book of the South American *Quiches*, "there was in the beginning nothing but water and the feathered serpent"; the first men that were created were destroyed by water.[2]

The *Zuñis* of New Mexico believed that when men first came upon the earth they were very wet, because there had been a time when "water was the world."[3] According to *Ovaherero* (a South-west African tribe) belief, "the old ones in Heaven once let the skies down with a run, but drew them up again when most of mankind had been drowned."[4] The *Zulus* say that from a bed

[1] Breysig, *op. cit.* pp. 35 ff.; Lang, *op. cit.* i. 176 ff.
[2] Lang, *op. cit.* i. p. 190.
[3] Ibid. ii. p. 86.
[4] Ibid. i. p. 171.

THE EVOLUTION OF THE MESSIANIC IDEA

of reeds all things originated [1]; so that probably here, too, the idea of a primeval watery element was once current. The *Ketshua* of ancient Peru taught that their god Huirakotsha made the moon and gave it light, and then placed it in the heavens, in order from there to rule over the seas and winds.[2] And so on; examples of a similar character could be given to a large extent from the works already cited, and from others. It is unnecessary to multiply examples; the few that have been given illustrate the contention that there is a general underlying idea among the most diverse races of men in a low stage of civilization, that a primeval watery element preceded all things, and that man's ills were somehow connected with it.

[1] Callaway, *Religious System of the Amazules*, p. 9 (1868).
[2] Breysig, *op. cit.* p. 57.

CHAPTER VII.

EXTENSIONS OF THE "TEHOM-MYTH."

THERE are reasons for believing that in the Old Testament there are to be found two "extensions" of the "Tehom-myth," viz.: (i) The Story of the Fall; (ii) The Story of the Flood—In the latter the myth of "Tehom-Rabbah" is to be differentiated from the legend, based on fact, of the Flood (*Hammabbūl*).

FROM the passages which were considered in Chapter V. the following points (among others) come out clearly. According to Amos ix. 3*b*, there dwells in the depth of the sea the "Serpent"; this sea-monster is spoken of as well known, and its actual existence was evidently believed in. The prophet Amos may have been using figurative language, but he must have been basing his teaching on pre-existing myth-material. This "Serpent"—it is "*the* Serpent" *par excellence*—injures men at Jahwe's command. There is reason to believe, as we saw, that it is only another designation for *Tehom*, or *Tehom Rabbah*. Further, it was pointed out (and this is, of course, taken for granted in the Amos passage just referred to), that *Tehom* (= Rahab)[1] was not finally annihilated in the great conflict with Jahwe. The "Serpent," who is also called "the coiling Serpent" and "the crooked Serpent," is

[1] According to Isaiah xxx. 7.

identified with Leviathan, the great sea-monster (Isa. xxvii. 1), who is to be devoured at some future time by demons. And, lastly, from Psalm lxxxix. 9-11, it is to be gathered that the "Sea" is personified in the "Serpent"; this might also be inferred from the Amos passage mentioned above; the *abode* of the "Serpent" might, by an easy transition, come even to be identified with the "Serpent," somewhat after the manner in which a "Bethel" came to be identified with the indwelling *Numen*.

i. Bearing these points in mind, it is possible that the *Story of the Fall*—or rather a more original form of it—contained an extension of the "Tehom-myth," or another scene in the great drama of the conflict between Jahwe and the primeval watery monster. The following considerations may perhaps be said to lend colour to this supposition.

In the story of the Fall (Gen. iii. 1-24), the Serpent plays a leading part; the section opens with the mention of him as, in reality, the most important of the *dramatis personæ* : the "subtil Serpent." One wonders whether at one time the words in verse 3, "than any beast of the field which the Lord God had made," were not absent from the text, for the whole presentation of the Serpent is so emphatically alien to the idea of his being one of "the beasts of the field," that

THE "SUBTIL SERPENT"

the words in question would be more appropriately omitted. In the same verse, after " and he said," the Septuagint inserts, " the Serpent," in which it is followed by the Syriac Version; strictly speaking, this is a more correct reading, as the text stands at present; its absence from the Hebrew suggests an incomplete addition, which has been rectified by the Septuagint. In this case the text would originally have run: " The Serpent was subtil (or crafty), and said to the woman," etc.

The question arises in what respect the Serpent was " crafty "; to suppose, as is usually done, that it was in order to bring about the " Fall," is to read later ideas into the narrative which originally cannot well have belonged to the spirit of it; for there is no word of enmity or grudge against the woman [1] or the man, the real *animus* is unmistakeably directed against Jahwe (see vv. 4, 5), and therefore the " craft " of the Serpent must originally have referred to his attempt to circumvent Jahwe. In the original story it may be surmised that the Serpent's " craft " consisted in his attempt to raise up a rival to Jahwe in the shape of the man; that he nearly succeeded is clear from verses 22-24: *And Jahwe-Elohim*

[1] This mention of the woman betrays a Jewish influence which must have been quite foreign to the original narrative.

THE EVOLUTION OF THE MESSIANIC IDEA

said, Behold, the man [1] *is become as one of us, to know good* [2] *and evil: and now lest he put forth his hand, and take also of the tree of life, and eat, and live for ever: therefore Jahwe-Elohim sent him forth from the garden of Eden, and placed at the east of the garden of Eden the Cherubim, and the flame of a sword which turned every way, to keep the way of the tree of life.*[3] The reason of the man being driven out of Eden had nothing to do with his disobedience to Jahwe, according to this passage, but was simply an act of prudence on the part of Jahwe in guarding against the danger of the man becoming equal to the gods (" us ") by eating of the fruit of the tree of life. The Serpent's craft, therefore, was exercised with the main idea of raising up a rival to Jahwe, and it consisted in the attempt to enable man, by eating of the fruit, to become as one of the gods.

The question then obviously arises, as to the reason of all this. We have seen above that the " Serpent " was identical with *Tehom* ; and the answer, therefore, is that, in the original form of

---

[1] In this genuinely antique portion of the narrative there is no mention of the woman.

[2] It may be mentioned in passing that if before partaking of the fruit the man did not " know good and evil," there can have been no question of a " Fall."

[3] The words, *To till the ground from whence he was taken, so he drove out the man,* cannot, for obvious reasons, have belonged to the original story. The text as it is has been worked over.

the narrative, it was an attempt on the part of *Tehom* to take vengeance on Jahwe for his victory in the great primeval conflict. That in this conflict *Tehom*, though overcome, was not annihilated has been pointed out several times. The fairly frequent notices that *Tehom* is not to be finally destroyed until some time in the distant future permits of the supposition that the conflict between him and Jahwe might from time to time have been renewed, indeed, this is almost stated in so many words in Psalm lxxxix. 10 (9), *Thou rulest the Sea when she rises up, thou stillest her waves when they roar.* Of the different forms in which, in the spirit of ancient myths, such renewed conflicts were represented, that preserved in Genesis iii. may have been one; it has, of course, been modified and worked over, and thus been adapted to later requirements.

ii. Still more decisive are the indications which point to the *Story of the Flood* as being an extension of the "Tehom-myth."[1] In Genesis vii. 11, the name "Tehom Rabbah" is directly applied to the Flood; in this verse mention is made of the "fountains" of "Tehom Rabbah," i.e. water from beneath, and water from the "windows of heaven," i.e. water from above;

[1] It is unnecessary for our present purpose to differentiate between the two accounts which have been interwoven in Genesis vi. 1–ix. 17, for both have made use of older material.

THE EVOLUTION OF THE MESSIANIC IDEA

this agrees precisely with the " cleaving in twain "[1] of *Tehom*, or as it is expressed in Genesis i. 7: *And God . . . divided the waters which were under the firmament from the waters which were above the firmament.* In a more original form of the myth, one may surmise that this part of the Flood Story recounted a yet further attempt on the part of *Tehom* to overcome Jahwe. A faint echo of the description of Jahwe's new victory is perhaps preserved in Genesis viii. 1–3: *And God caused a wind (ruaḥ) to pass over the earth, and the waters assuaged; the fountains also of Tehom and the windows of heaven were stopped, and the rain from heaven was restrained . . .*; the thought recalls the way in which the first attack of Jahwe upon *Tehom* was made—according to the highly spiritualized form of the account in Genesis i. 2: *And the earth was waste and void, and darkness was upon the face of Tehom, and the spirit (ruaḥ) of God brooded upon the waters.*

It is thus possible that in some earlier form of the "Tehom-myth" more than one scene was recounted. There was the first great conflict in which *Tehom* was overcome, but not destroyed; secondly, *Tehom* sought by craft to enable Jahwe's greatest creation, man, to become divine, and (presumably) to aid *Tehom* in his struggle with Jahwe; again *Tehom* (the "Serpent") is worsted; thirdly, a new onslaught is

[1] See p. 61.

"THE SEA (*TEHOM*) IS NO MORE"

made by *Tehom*, who covers the whole earth with his waters, and by this means seeks to destroy Jahwe—Jahwe's abode, as will be noticed below, is located on the earth ; [1]—and once more *Tehom* is beaten off. That possibly other conflicts were conceived of as taking place has been already mentioned. The final destruction is again and again referred to as an event which will take place in the distant future. That consummation is reached ultimately; in the Apocalypse, xxi. 1, it is recorded: *And I saw a new heaven and a new earth ; for the first heaven and the first earth are passed away*; AND THE SEA IS NO MORE. The intimate connexion between this and the Person of the Messiah is clearly shown in this chapter of the Apocalypse. The words in verse 10, *And he carried me away in the spirit to a mountain great and high*, are also, as will be noticed in a later chapter, intimately connected with our subject.

* * * * *

It remains to be pointed out that the story of the Deluge was originally quite distinct from what has just been referred to. *Tehom Rabbah* (" The Great Deep ") and *The Deluge* (*Hammabbūl*) are two things quite distinct ; with the latter we have nothing to do here. That they

---

[1] That the Ark rested on a mountain (Gen. viii. 4) is significant in view of what is said below concerning the Mount of God.

have been inextricably mixed up in the Old Testament lies almost in the nature of things; for when a mythological drama like the "*Tehom-myth*" has some points of affinity with a tradition like that of the Flood (which, it seems highly probable, has some basis in fact), it is inevitable that one should reflect upon the other. The very reason given for the sending of the Flood (*Hammabbūl*) is founded upon what is, beyond all question, mythology (Gen. vi. 1–8); and mythological *traits* are in evidence throughout the two Biblical accounts.[1] Nevertheless, that the Deluge (*Hammabbūl*), as distinct from an episode in the "*Tehom-myth*," has a basis in fact, seems indubitable, though the reasons for this belief cannot be gone into here.

[1] Cf. the writer's article "The Dove with the Olive Leaf" in the *Expos. Times* for May, 1907, pp. 377 ff.

CHAPTER VIII.

THE " JAHWE-MYTH."

A MORE appropriate name would be "Saviour-myth" or "*Heilbringer*-myth"—The original form of the myth—The "Heilbringer" a Hero who overcame the primeval watery monster, and who also brought temporal blessings to his people—Some Old Testament passages considered: Gen. ii. 5–7, 19; Isa. li. 9–11; Ps. lxv. 7, 8; Ps. lxxiv. 12–17; Ps. lxxxix. 6–19; Ps. civ. 5–9—These passages, again, are only examples.

[LITERATURE: In addition to the works indicated at the head of Chap. V, Gressmann, *Der Ursprung der israelitisch-jüdischen Eschatologie* (1905).]

As already remarked, the term "Jahwe-myth" is used in order to denote that the Israelite name of God was attached to a pre-existing myth, and not as implying that Jahwe-belief among the Israelites is to be regarded as coming under the category of mythology.

This myth, under varying names, is, like the "Tehom-myth," world-wide; a more appropriate name for it would perhaps be "Saviour-myth," excepting that, owing to the present connotation of the word "Saviour," the name might be misunderstood. The most fitting title would unquestionably be the German, "Heilbringer."

According to the present theory, the root-idea

THE EVOLUTION OF THE MESSIANIC IDEA

of this myth is the outcome of the innate human characteristic of dependence on a higher power, the natural looking for someone to help in view of present stress; and therefore the "Leitmotif," in all the many varying forms of it, is that of the "Saviour-Hero," or "Heilbringer," coming to help. As here maintained, the earliest form of this myth, which must originally have been of the simplest character, represented the "Saviour-Hero" as delivering men from the power of the cruel watery monster, who was the cause of so many of the direst evils of which men were the victims. But the necessary development of all myths would soon have caused extensions and modifications of the original underlying idea, and the activity of the "Saviour-Hero," or "Heilbringer," as we had perhaps better call him, would be conceived of not merely as warding off evil, but as also bringing good. Having exhibited his power in so manifest a way as to be the bulwark, for men, against the onslaughts of the cruel primeval monster, it would have been an easy and natural transition if he came to be looked upon as the " Bringer of blessings " of all kinds; the most prized possessions would come to be attributed to his beneficent activity. And if the theory here advocated be correct, that this dependence on a higher power is an elemental characteristic

MANY FORMS OF THE "JAHWE-MYTH"

in man, then the root-idea which gave birth to this myth is common to man, and we shall expect to find the myth appearing in the most diverse quarters, modified in character and different in detail, of course, according to the varying mental mould of those among whom it took its many original forms. So that here, too, one original form of the myth is regarded as out of the question; for one root-idea, viz., the need of a helper, expressed itself in numbers of different myths, each form, in the first instance, being original. To be sure, when in the various human branches of one original stock differing forms of the same myth are found, it is reasonable to suppose that the diverse forms are variations from one original; and even distinct races will undoubtedly have influenced the forms and contents of each others' myths through contact and intermingling, as in the case of Aryans and Semites. But these are later developments; in the first instance, it is maintained, there were only original forms, and many of them.

It has already been said that, owing to the fact that the "Jahwe-myth" has been so inextricably interwoven with the "Tehom-myth" in the Old Testament, some of the points to be considered have already been touched upon in the preceding chapters; these slight repetitions are, however, unavoidable.

THE EVOLUTION OF THE MESSIANIC IDEA

In dealing with the echoes of this myth in the Old Testament it is realized that there is a great danger of attempting to extract from some passages matter which they do not really contain; the desire to find references which go to substantiate a theory offers considerable temptation to the play of the imagination. For this reason a number of passages which might quite conceivably be regarded as *à propos* have not been utilized; only such are brought into requisition concerning which it may be said with reasonable certainty that they contain archaic elements.

(*a*) **Genesis ii. 5–7, 19:** *And when as yet no plant of the field was in the earth, and no herb of the field had sprouted because Jahwe-Elohim had not caused it to rain upon the earth—and there was no man to till the ground—a fountain welled forth out of the earth* (cf. Septuagint) *and watered all the surface of the earth. Then Jahwe-Elohim formed man of the dust of the ground, and blew into his nostrils the breath of life; and thus man became a living being. . . . So Jahwe-Elohim formed, further,* (cf. Samaritan and Septuagint) *out of the ground all the beasts of the field and all the birds of the heavens; and he brought them to the man to see what he would call them, and whatsoever the man— the living soul* (as in ver. 7)—*called each, that was its name.*

This (Jahwistic) passage is acknowledged on

GENESIS II. 5-7, 19

all hands to be considerably earlier in date than the parallel account in Genesis i. 1 ff. One must recognize in it some genuinely antique conceptions. The existence of the earth is presupposed before the appearance of Jahwe : this accords with the belief that the primeval watery monster, *Tehom*, was in the world first, for, by common consent, he was there before the earth was. The earth was, no doubt, conceived of as chaotic, but nevertheless as existent before Jahwe came forth as the Benefactor of the human race, and brought to man what he required. It is worth noting that even in the later Creation account the older belief of the earth's existence before God began His work upon it has not been wholly eradicated ; for the earth, described as *Tohu wabohu* (" waste and void "), can scarcely have been conceived of as God's work, of which it is so often said, *And God saw that it was good*. A second very old-world idea is that of a mass of water underneath the earth. Gunkel, quoting Holzinger, has an interesting note on the word used ('$\bar{E}d$) for this water (v. 6), he says : " The sense of ' Flood ' (for this word) is to be preferred on account of the verb which is used, viz. *hishqah* ; mist may indeed be said to moisten the earth, but not to *water* it. This rare word ('$\bar{E}d$) will probably have been a technical term, belonging specially to this Creation story. . . . If the translation ' spring ' or ' flood ' be correct,

then the *'Ed* must be pictured as a world-stream, whence all the waters on the earth are derived. The idea of the origin of the *'Ed* from dry land is paralleled by that of the birth of the Sea from the womb of the Earth (Job xxxviii. 8). Very significant is the fact that it is not said that Jahwe created this *'Ed*; on the contrary, strictly speaking, this is excluded, for, from the point of view of these verses, the condition of the world *before* Jahwe's entry upon the scene is described in 5 and 6, whereas Jahwe's ' creative acts ' are only recounted in the seventh and following verses. It seems clear, therefore, though the fact shines out but dimly through these words, that the conception of the *'Ed* was that of some mighty power, the existence of which was not due to Jahwe ; a conception which is certainly extremely antique." [1]
And thirdly, the way man is represented as having been created is exceedingly *naïve* ; the picture of Jahwe forming man with the dust of the earth is precisely paralleled by that of the potter making a vessel, for the word used (*yaṣar*) is a technical term for the potter's way of working ; e.g., Isaiah xxix. 16 : *Shall the potter (hayyoṣer) be counted as clay, that the thing should say of him that made it, He made me not ; and the thing framed (yēṣer) say of him that framed it (yōṣᵉro),*

[1] *Genesis*, p. 4.

ISAIAH LI. 9-11

He hath no understanding? (cf. Isa. xli. 25; Jer. xviii. 4, 6); it is of interest to notice that not infrequently this picture of a potter framing a vessel is used in connexion with Jahwe and His people, so in Isaiah xxvii. 11; xliii. 1, 7; xliv. 21, etc.; it is the same expression which is used in reference to the creation of other things, e.g. of the mountains (Amos iv. 13); of the earth itself (Isa. xlv. 18; Ps. xcv. 5); of the eye of man (Ps. xciv. 9); of the locust (Amos vii. 1). Moreover, the same word is used in Genesis ii. 19, of the " forming " of every beast of the field, etc. The verses before us, therefore, represent Jahwe as the maker (" Former," *yōser*; not " Creator," *bōrē'*) of man, and as the Benefactor who brought to man great blessings, i.e. primarily, what he required for food. This is the genuine " Heilbringer " conception, and it is one which, as will be seen below, is quite parallel to what is found among other peoples regarding a great Benefactor of their race, who lived long ago, and who brought them great blessings in the shape of material gifts, or, at all events, gifts which conduced to their comfort.

(*b*) **Isaiah li. 9–11:** Part of this passage has already been considered in another connexion;[1] in the echoes perhaps of an ancient hymn, the " Arm of Jahwe "[2] is bidden to rouse itself " as in days of old, as in ages long since past "; and it is

[1] See pp. 50 ff.   [2] See pp. 100 f.

recalled that in those bygone ages Jahwe clave in pieces Rahab, the Dragon. There is a truly antique ring about those words, especially when one remembers that the words *Tehom Rabbah*, *Yām, Rahab* are really proper names, and are applied, as we have seen above, to the great sea-monster who was believed to have been supreme in power in the remote ages long ago. The whole of these verses may well be regarded as an adaptation, and as having been placed within contexts with which, originally, they had nothing to do. It will be seen that on reading verses 12 ff. immediately after verse 8, the intervening verses (the passage before us) are not missed. At all events, it cannot be questioned that the mental atmosphere of the verses in question differs entirely from that of those that precede and follow ; verses 9-11 break the thought-connexion of the passage ; in verses 7, 8, there are two main thoughts—(i) the people are bidden not to " fear the reproach of men or to be dismayed at their revilings," for they are to be destroyed ; and (ii) God's righteousness and salvation endure for ever ; these two thoughts are developed in verses 12 ff., where in continuation of (ii) it says : " I, even I, am he that comforteth you," while in continuation of (i) it goes on : " Who art thou, that thou art afraid of man that shall die . . ."; so that verses 9-11, which deal with quite a different set of ideas, and speak of a past event, interrupt the sequence of thought of the preceding and following verses, and contain a reference which can only be considered à propos, in any sense, to their contexts by regarding them as an adaptation. What Gunkel says in another connexion is well illustrated here: "It is the common fate of ancient stories which have been preserved in a later form, that certain *traits* which at one time, viz. in their earlier, original connexion, were perfectly comprehensible, have lost that connexion in the more recent form in which the stories have been handed down. These ancient *traits*, fragments of an earlier whole, lacking as they do their proper connexion in the present account, and scarcely comprehensible because of their having been wrested from the thought-sequence of the original writer, betray to the expert the existence, together with some isolated fragments, of an earlier form of the story as it lies before him." [1] We have here, that is to say, the echo of an ancient myth in which a great hero (with whom in later days Jahwe was identified) came forth as a champion, and saved men from a cruel enemy.

(c) **Psalm lxv. 7, 8 (6, 7):**

Who arrangeth the mountains by His strength,
  Girded with might;
Who stilleth the raging of the seas,
  The roaring of their waves.

[1] *Chaos und Schöpfung,* p. 6.

THE EVOLUTION OF THE MESSIANIC IDEA

The third member of verse 8: *And the tumult of the peoples*, does not seem to belong to the psalm; the words spoil the parallelism of ideas, and disturb the verse-balance. The reference in the passage to the Creation and to the conflict with *Tehom* are clearly discernible; a distinct community of ideas seems to exist between this passage and Jeremiah x. 12, 13; the latter is worth quoting:

He hath made (the Septuagint reads: "The Lord hath made") *the earth by his power, he hath established the world (Tēbēl) by his wisdom, and by his understanding hath he stretched out the heavens;* (the following words: "When he uttereth his voice," are omitted by the Septuagint); *there is a tumult of the waters in the heavens, and he causeth vapours to ascend from the end of the earth; lightnings for the rain he maketh, and he bringeth forth wind* (the Septuagint reads: "light") *out of his treasures.*

These identical words occur again in Isaiah li. 15, 16, a fact which strengthens the supposition that they formed part of the pre-existing myth-material to which reference has already been made; possibly Psalm lxv. 7, 8 belonged to the same hymn from which the Jeremiah passage has been taken. In each case it is to the distant past that reference is made. In the passage before us (ver. 8) the words: *That stilleth the raging of the seas,*

PSALM LXV. 9, 10

recall the words in Psalm lxxxix. 10 : *Thou stillest her waves when they roar* [1] (cf. the Septuagint). Of the existence of ancient *traits* in this psalm there can, therefore, be no doubt ; the significance of this is, however, seen in the fact that the divine-human hero is identified with the Bringer of Blessings ; verses 9–14 are, no doubt, late, but the idea which they contain of the divine-human [2] " Heilbringer " bringing them material blessings must be very ancient ; particularly noticeable in this connexion are the words in verse 9 (8 in R.V.) :

> *They also that dwell in the uttermost parts of the earth are afraid of thy tokens ;*
> *Thou makest the outgoings of the morning and evening to rejoice ;*

and in verse 10 (9 in R.V.) :

> *Thou visitest the earth, and waterest it,*
> *Thou greatly enrichest it ;*
> *The river of God is full of water ;*
> *Thou providest them corn, when thou hast so prepared the earth.*

Many of the ideas which these passages reveal are exceedingly *naïve* (though this is not so apparent in the English as in the original version), and must

[1] On this word see above, Chapter V., under Psalm lxxxix. 9–11, pp. 55 f.

[2] Divine as Creator, human as Dragon-slayer—the mixing up of the ideas is, of course, late.

THE EVOLUTION OF THE MESSIANIC IDEA

be very ancient, so that although the psalm as we now have it is of late date, comparatively speaking, yet it embodies elements which must go back to an immense antiquity. The same thing is found in parts of the books of Isaiah and of Job. This preservation of ancient elements in poetical literature can be paralleled by analogous examples among other peoples. In the present connexion the significance of this is obvious.

(*d*) **Psalm lxxiv. 12–17**: The first four verses of the passage have already been considered;[1] their antique character is evidenced by the fact that they refer to something that happened long ago; the existence of the primeval sea-monster who was overcome by God (Jahwe) is taken to be well known; the whole scene of action is placed in the distant past ("of old," v. 12). It is, therefore, with the thought of this past deliverance, resulting in the bringing of "salvation" ("working salvations"; $y^eshu\'ah=$"salvation" is used primarily of external deliverance) upon the earth (land ?),[2] that verses 16, 17 are connected:

> 16. *Thine is the day, yea, thine is the night; thou hast set in order again the sun and the moon* (cf. the Septuagint);

[1] See pp. 53 f.
[2] "Land," i.e. a restricted area, is perhaps more exact, in view of "my King," which would imply a particular country, but see below.

PSALM LXXIV. 12-17

17. *Thou hast set all the borders of the earth; summer and winter, thou hast fashioned them.*

In 16b the LXX^B rendering is to be preferred on account of its better correspondence with the first half of the verse; the MSS. ℵ$^{c.a}$T read " Light and Sun," a literal rendering of the Hebrew, which does not strike one as original. In verse 17, *yaṣar* (LXX^B: "made," but ℵ$^{c.a}$T: "formed"), used of "forming" the seasons, strikes an antique note (cf. above on this word).[1]

In these two verses (in which one must, of course, assume the same spirit as in the preceding ones, 12-15) Jahwe is He who arranged day and night, set in order again the sun and the moon—the word used in the Greek version suggests the idea of *rectifying*—fixed the borders of the earth—here there is assuredly an echo of Genesis i. 6, 7—and fashioned summer and winter (*hōrēph*, strictly speaking, "autumn"). These things were real blessings to man, the "salvations" referred to in verse 12, and the mention of them in connexion with Jahwe, presents Him in the true "Heilbringer" character. It is scarcely necessary to add that these verses can be read and understood in the sense of Jahwe's Creatorship in the highest conception of the term; and it is likely enough that the psalm, as we now have it, was written by one who did understand it in

[1] See pp. 88 f.

THE EVOLUTION OF THE MESSIANIC IDEA

this sense; but it is contended that in this psalm use has been made of some already existing material —of hoary antiquity in its original form—in which less exalted conceptions of Jahwe were present, and in which He appeared as a "Bringer of Blessings" in the "Heilbringer" sense. This contention seems justified on account of the exceedingly antique notes sounded in verses 12-15. The whole passage may therefore be regarded as an adaptation of earlier material.

(*e*) **Psalm lxxxix. 6-19 (5-18):** Here again the verses (9-11, A.V. 8-10) which speak of Jahwe's conflict with the primeval sea-monster, and which therefore testify to the high antiquity of the material used, have already been considered.[1] But there are other verses in the passage which also strike notes of a very old-world character. In verses 6-8 we read:

6. *The heavens did praise thy wondrous act, Jahwe: Thy steadfastness also* (was praised) *in the company of the holy ones* (i.e. angels);

7. *For who in the sky is comparable* (cf. Ps. xl. 6, (5)) *to Jahwe? Who is like Jahwe among the 'b'nei 'elim'?*

8. *El is terrible in the secret council of his holy ones* (i.e. angels); *great, and fear-inspiring towards all that are round about him.*

[1] See pp. 55 f.

PSALM LXXXIX. 6-19

In verse 6 the Hebrew text speaks only of one wondrous act ($pil'ăkā=$" thy wondrous act "), though the plural is used in the Septuagint, Vulgate and Syriac; but the Hebrew here seems more correct, because the " wondrous act "—and it was *sui generis*—is specified in verse 11, *thou hast humbled Rahab, as one that is dishonoured, with thy mighty arm hast thou scattered thine enemies;* the "wondrous act" was, therefore, the victory of Jahwe over the primeval sea-monster. The "holy ones" ($q^e doshīm$) are evidently angels (cf. Deut. xxxiii. 3; Zech. xiv. 5; Job. v. 1; xv. 15; Dan. iv. 10, 14, 20; viii. 13); in verse 8 of this psalm Jahwe is represented as One of the secret council of the angels who are constantly round about Him. Originally the differentiation between Jahwe and the angels was one of degree rather than of kind. This is clearly brought out in the earliest of the Biblical documents (J), e.g. in Genesis xviii.; here Jahwe is one of the three who are represented as companions, Jahwe taking the leading position, though equal honour is shown to all; that the two men with Jahwe are angels is directly asserted in xix. 1, where we are told that they went to Sodom, after it had been said in xviii. 33 that Jahwe "went His way." Moreover, Jahwe's original identity with an angel, according to early Hebrew conception, is distinctly seen by comparing, e.g. such a passage as Exodus iii. 2, with verse 4 ; in the former verse it is " the angel of the Lord " who appears in the burning bush, in the latter it is God ; there is, furthermore, direct identification in Genesis xvi. 10, 13 ; xxi. 17 ff. In the earliest document in which angels are mentioned (J) they appear only by twos or threes, in the later document (E) they appear in greater numbers (Gen. xxviii. 12 ; xxxii. 1, 2) ; this is just what is to be expected, for J, the earlier document, represents Jahwe in a less exalted form, who Himself comes down on earth, and personally carries out His purposes ; by degrees, however, more exalted conceptions of Him obtain, especially as the conception of His characteristic of holiness becomes realized, so that His presence among men comes to appear incongruous and unfitting, and His activity is delegated to His messengers, or angels.[1] The facts here stated have an important bearing on the " Heilbringer " character of Jahwe.

The points enumerated above, especially when read in connexion with verses 9–11, to which attention has already been drawn in Chapter V. are sufficient to show the antique *traits* with which this part of the psalm abounds. This must be borne in mind in referring briefly to verses 12–19.

[1] See the present writer's art. " Angels," in Hastings' *Smaller Dictionary of the Bible.*

PSALM LXXXIX. 6-19

12. *Thine are the Heavens, yea, thine is the earth; Tēbēl and its fulness, thou didst found it.*

13. *North and South, thou didst create them; Tabor and Hermon shout at thy name.*

14. *Thine is the arm, with thee* (cf. the Peshitta Version) *is might; thine hand is strong, glorious thy right hand.*

15. *Righteousness and Justice are the foundation of thy throne; mercy and faithfulness go before thy face.*

16. *Blessed are the people that know the "shout": Jahwe, in the light of thy countenance they shall walk;*

17. *In thy name shall they rejoice all the day: and in thy righteousness they shall shout for joy;*

18. *For the glory of their strength art thou: and by thy favour our horn shall be exalted;*

19. *For unto Jahwe belongeth our shield: yea, unto the holy one of Israel, our King.*

There are, firstly, a few words in these verses which require a brief examination. In verse 12, *Tēbēl*, as is implied in the following word, *m'lo'ah* (="its fulness"), means the world from the point of view of its productivity (cf. the words *y'būl*, "produce of the soil" (Deut. xi. 17), and *būl*,

THE EVOLUTION OF THE MESSIANIC IDEA

" produce " (Isa. xliv. 19; Job xl. 20), both of which come from the same root, (*yabal*); there does not seem to be sufficient justification for the meaning which is usually attached to it, as being equivalent to the Greek *oikoumenē*, " the inhabited world." *Tēbēl* is always used without the article, and is therefore very ancient, probably a mythological term; though in later usage it is often found as parallel to *'ereṣ*. But occurring as it does here, in a passage which, as it is, is full of ancient *traits*, the word must be regarded as affording further evidence of mythological elements. In verse 13 the mention of the " North " as having been created by Jahwe is full of significant interest; Paradise, the " garden of Jahwe," was located in the North (cf. Gen. ii. 10 ff. and Isa. xiv. 13 : *And thou saidst in thy heart: I will ascend into Heaven, I will exalt my throne above the stars of God; and I will sit upon the mount of assembly in the farthest North*), it was there that the " company of the holy ones " (ver. 6) dwelt; this corresponds to the " mount of assembly " in Isaiah xi. 13 (see further on this point under Chap. X). In verse 14 the " Arm " of Jahwe is again mentioned—the antique conception contained in this anthropomorphism has already been touched upon;[1] parallel to it are His " Hand " and His " Right Hand "; in each case it is probable that the

[1] See pp. 89 f.

thought of Jahwe's Sword was in the first instance connected with it, for as a rule, when these expressions occur it is a question of Jahwe opposing or conquering peoples in battle (e.g. Exod. xv. 6-16; Isa. lii. 10; Ps. xliv. 3; lxxix. 11; cxviii. 15). Gressmann, in commenting on the verse before us, pointedly remarks: " It is hardly permissible to speak of ' metaphor ' here, as the picture is not complete, but only of a fragmentary character. The Arm of Jahwe must at one time have been conceived of as something actual, otherwise it would not have been spoken about. But in the writings of the Old Testament as we now have them the idea of an actual Hand is no more present. . . . We are dealing with phrases which originally described something material but which later on were no longer so; in the first instance they were used in reference to a God who accorded victory, and who gave help." [1]. In verse 16 occur the words rendered: " Blessed are the people that know the ' shout ' " ; this is the most obvious way of rendering the Hebrew *t'ru'ah* and Septuagint *alalagmon ;* there does not seem sufficient justification, as far as this passage is concerned, for either the R.V. " joyful sound " or the R.V.[mg.] " trumpet sound." Although the proposed rendering does not, apparently, give any sense at first sight, it might

[1] *Op. cit.* p. 122.

do so if it could be shown that the words contain a mythological echo; and perhaps this is possible. That the whole passage (6–19) teems with archaic conceptions will scarcely be doubted, so that a phrase like this, which seems meaningless as it stands, may well conceal some mythological reference. In some earlier verses of this psalm (6–8) mention is made of Jahwe's " Holy ones " who praised His " wondrous act," and who formed Jahwe's " secret council "; the " b'nei 'elim" too are spoken of, they are probably the same as the " Holy ones "; the wondrous act which they praised was Jahwe's victory over Rahab (*Tehom*). Now on turning to Job xxxviii. 4–20, we find a reference to the first beginnings of things (4–6), and of the " shutting up of the sea with doors," and of setting " bars and bolts " (8–10; cf. what was said above about the " bolts ");[1] here, therefore, there is indubitably the thought of Jahwe's victory over *Tehom*, just as there is in the psalm before us (9–11); but in Job xxxviii. 7 occur the words: *And all the sons of God shouted;* the shout must, in the original form of the account, have been in consequence of Jahwe's victory over *Tehom*; just as in the Chaldæan account, after Merodach's victory over Tiamat, the gods shouted: " Merodach is King "; noteworthy, too, is the

[1] See pp. 61 f.

similarity of ideas between verses 7, 8 of our psalm and the words on Tablet IV of the Chaldæan account:

> "Thou," they cried, "art glorious among the great gods;
> Thy lot is peerless, thy word exalted!
> Merodach, thou art glorious among the great gods,
> Thy lot is peerless, thy word exalted!"[1]

It is, then, quite possible that the words, *Blessed are the people that know the shout*, and the "shouting of the sons of God" in Job xxxviii. 7, refer to the same thing; it will be remembered that the "b'nei 'elim" are referred to a few verses previously in our psalm. This would therefore be an admirable illustration of Gunkel's words, quoted above: "It is the common fate of ancient stories which have been preserved in a later form, that certain *traits* which at one time, viz. in their earlier, original connexion, were perfectly comprehensible, have lost that connexion in the more recent form in which the stories have been handed down."

The main points, therefore, in Psalm lxxxix. 6–19 which concern us are, that it contains many ancient elements, that Jahwe's victory over Rahab (*Tehom*) is directly referred to, that through this victory the heavens and the earth with its fulness became Jahwe's, and that therefore the "horn" of His people shall be exalted.

[1] Ball, *Light from the East*, pp. 7, 8 (1899).

THE EVOLUTION OF THE MESSIANIC IDEA

It is not necessary to do more than merely mention the fact that the expression " exalting the horn " is a synonym for enjoying *material* prosperity. This passage, as regards its archaic elements, therefore, offers a clear representation of Jahwe in the character of " Heilbringer."

(*f*) One more example, and likewise a very instructive one, may be given; it is Psalm civ., which illustrates admirably the way in which ancient ideas were adapted to the requirements of later ages. Verses 5–9 are the first to be considered—although the previous verses are certainly not lacking in antique echoes :

> *He founded the earth upon her pillars : she shall not move for evermore ;*
> *Tehom covered her like a garment : upon the hills the waters stood.*
> *At thy rebuke they fled : at the voices of thy thunder they fled in terror.*
> *Mountains rose up, valleys sank down into the place which thou didst fix for them ;*
> *A bound thou didst set (which) they may not overstep : they may not return to cover the earth.*

Here the reference to the ancient myth of Jahwe's victory over *Tehom* is too obvious to require any insisting upon (cf. too verse 26 ; another antique *trait* is found in verse 32). The

PSALM CIV. 5-9

rest of the psalm deals with the many blessings which Jahwe has given to His people; all the good things that men enjoy have been given by Him. It is the combination of this latter—in other contexts an ordinary and natural acknowledgement and gratitude to Jahwe—with the clear reference to the "Tehom-myth," which suggests the idea that this remaining portion of the psalm contains a reminiscence, extended, adapted and highly embellished, of an ancient " Heilbringer "-myth, which is now utilized in the interests of Jahwe-worship. This idea is emphasized when one notices that through almost the whole of the psalm there is an enumeration of the blessings which Jahwe has given to His people, blessings which are all material in character—the fruits of the earth, wine, oil, bread, etc.; the moon and the sun. There are, of course, other elements in this psalm which point to ideas of a later time; but the fact of importance is that the ancient myth, according to which a "Saviour-Hero" (" Heilbringer ") slew the primeval watery monster, and then became a Benefactor to his people by bringing them many material blessings, forms the original basis of the psalm; this " Heilbringer "-myth was then first adapted to Jahwe-worship, and celebrated in song, it may be, for ages, before it became embodied in this hymn of praise—which is, of

THE EVOLUTION OF THE MESSIANIC IDEA

course, in its present form, of quite late date. There are, very probably, other psalms in which, originally, a similar theme was treated, and then adapted to the more advanced religious ideas of later periods—so perhaps Psalm xciii., for example —but the original colouring has become so paled that it is only here and there that it can be observed.

In these few passages that have been considered we have, as will be generally acknowledged, fragments of literature which have gone through more than one process of editing; compiled from written sources which, as literature, must have had a history behind them, and which were themselves adaptations of previously existing material which embodied some of the traditional beliefs held for ages, and which even during this oral stage must have undergone many modifications—is it to be wondered at that only broken remnants have survived? The " Heilbringer "-myth, of which some traces, it is hoped, have been indicated in the passages just discussed, must have been subject to great variations during its vicissitudes within the Semitic area, extending, as it assuredly did, over a period of time which must be reckoned by millenniums; and therefore it is not to be expected that these passages should offer much more than *echoes* of the distant past. But those echoes seem, at any rate, to reveal

THE "JAHWE-MYTH"

the root-idea, viz. that a "Saviour-Hero" subdued the primeval watery monster; he then formed men and became their Benefactor or "Heilbringer" in that he gave them material blessings. This figure, at first probably only an indistinct Ancestor-hero, gradually assumed a superhuman character, and was regarded as a leader among the "b'nei 'elim" above; finally the God of Israel, Jahwe, became identified with him.

Just as in the "Tehom-myth" the central root-idea is belief in the existence of a primeval watery monster who was regarded as the embodiment of evil, in the sense of harm-doing, so in the case of the "Jahwe-myth" the central root-idea is belief in the existence of a great Divine-Human Helper, who, by subduing the Dragon, prepared the way for the presence of men on the earth; these men he made, and furnished them with material blessings. Later ages recognized in him—Jahwe.

CHAPTER IX.

THE "JAHWE(*HEILBRINGER*)-MYTH" AMONG OTHER PEOPLES.

The underlying conception of the "Jahwe-myth" not the exclusive possession of the Hebrews—Examples of "*Heilbringer*-myths": Babylonian, Egyptian, Indian, Zoroastrian, Greek, Algonquin, Iroquois, Thlinkeet, Bakaïri, Namaqua, Zulu, Bushmen, Zuñi, Mayas, Ahts—These only a few examples out of a great many that exist—The "Heilbringer" a personality who is half-human, half-divine.

[Literature: As above, (Chap. VI.), especially the cited works of Breysig and Lang.]

As in the case of the *Tehom*-myth, so here, it will be necessary to try and show that in its essence the underlying idea of the *Jahwe*-myth was not the exclusive possession of the Hebrews. When it is found that in the Old Testament form of the myth there are certain elements which may be paralleled by other forms of an (originally) similar myth, which are known to exist among many other peoples, there is some justification for the inference that in the Old Testament we have but one of the many expressions of a root-idea which was, in the first instance, common to man; and thus the theory of a single original form of the myth will, on account of the widely separated areas in which the same root-idea finds

THE "HEILBRINGER"

expression, be excluded. The root-idea which underlay the earliest forms of the myth, which for convenience' sake we still designate "Jahwe"-myth, was the feeling of dependence on some stronger power which men naturally feel; this power was, of course, far from being conceived of as divine; it was super-human in the sense of being physically stronger and cleverer (this word is used advisedly, in preference to "wiser") than men; it was also super-human on account of its supposed control over what we now call the powers of nature. It is necessary to guard oneself against using the word "supernatural" here, for to early man the idea of there being anything supernatural had not yet arisen. But in other respects this power was a human one in the most literal sense of the word.

Among the Israelites conceptions of a greatly developed character did not hinder very *naïve* ideas concerning Jahwe being entertained; as is well known, anthropomorphisms abound in the Old Testament; and terms are applied to Him which would be quite unfitting in such a spiritual worship as the religion of Jahwe, unless these terms had become time-honoured. That is to say, the terms in question, or their equivalent, must have been used in reference to some strong Hero for ages before that Hero came to be called Jahwe; and for long after he came to be so called, the

THE EVOLUTION OF THE MESSIANIC IDEA

conceptions held concerning him must have been much lower even than some of the less exalted ones which are met with in the Old Testament. So that when we find it said, for example, *And God* [1] *made two great lights*, it is quite permissible to believe that in an earlier stage this statement was expressed in a less exalted form. To men in a less advanced stage of culture the *dictum* that God created the world out of nothing could mean nothing at all, the idea was simply impossible; they would ask "Whence?" and "How?" And they would not be satisfied without an answer.

* * * * *

We proceed now to give as tersely as possible some instances of "Heilbringer"-myths among peoples differing from each other in many ways; that these instances—as was the case in the chapter on the *Tehom*-myth—could be greatly multiplied, goes without saying.

Among the *Babylonians* the figure of Marduk appears unmistakeably in the character of "Heilbringer." He comes forth as the champion of the gods, and subdues Tiamat; this is preparatory to the appearance of man on earth. Marduk forms

---

[1] It is immaterial what name for the deity is used, whether Elohim or Jahwe, for the *personality* is the same.

BABYLONIAN "HEILBRINGER"

men out of clay and the blood of gods [1]; they look to him as their Helper. In the fifth Creation Tablet we are told of how Marduk (Bel-Merodach) formed the stars, and arranged various other things for man's benefit:

He formed a station for the great gods;
Stars like unto themselves, the *Lu-mashi* (i.e. the "shining flock"), he stationed there.
He appointed the year, dividing it into seasons;
The twelve months—three stars for each he stationed,
From the day when the year sets out unto the end thereof. . . . . . .
Nannaru he made shine forth, made him overseer of night;
He appointed him, a being of night, to determine days:
Every month unfailingly with crescent-crown make division (?) ! [2]

" What else the Tablet related, after the account of the celestial arrangements, we do not know. Zimmern supposes that it went on to tell of the creation of dry land and sea, and perhaps also of vegetation." [3]

Marduk appears also as the helper of men in distress and their healer in sickness, and he it is who "awakens men from the dead." [4] In a

[1] Schrader-Zimmern, *Keilinschriften* (3rd ed.) pp. 496 ff., cited by Breysig, *op. cit.* p. 107. "The creation of man from dust or clay is a belief among the Maoris, Samoans, Pelewans, Tahitians, Dyaks, Kumis, Kaffirs, Pimas, and Eskimo." Crawley, *The Tree of Life*, p. 64 (1905).
[2] Ball, *op. cit.* p. 12.
[3] *Ibid.*
[4] Jeremias, *op. cit.* p. 30.

text in the *Šurpu* series, he is spoken of as follows:

> Thou art able to heal the sick,
> Thou art able to raise up him that is fallen,
> Thou art able to succour the weak,
> Thou art able to avert an unkind fate.[1]

The whole subject of Marduk as "Heilbringer" is dealt with by Breysig, *op. cit.* pp. 102-117.

In seeking for the figure of a "Heilbringer" in ancient *Egyptian* belief one is faced with great difficulties; the religion of Egypt is so extraordinarily complicated, one is lost in such a maze of semi-animal deities, there is such a throwing hither and thither of attributes among these various deities, and there is such a mixture of deep philosophy with the most crass absurdities that, excepting for a specialist on the subject, it is impossible to gain any sufficiently clear ideas for the purpose of presenting a reasonably certain instance of "Heilbringer."

Perhaps the greatest of these difficulties is as Breysig puts it: "The enormous variety of forms in the Egyptian Pantheon," and especially the "blending together, the dissolving, or metamorphosis, of particular divine characters;" he goes on to say: "This has been brought about, as in the case of Babylonia, through the purely political

[1] Zimmern, *Beiträge zur Kenntniss der Babylonischen Religion*, quoted in Jeremias, *op. cit.* p. 31.

EGYPTIAN "HEILBRINGER"

action of welding together into a single kingdom many provinces which were originally independent. The gods of these various localities shared the same fate as the districts themselves; the origin of the multiplicity of gods which is observable in the later history—not due to religious causes, but, in reality, to the exigencies of State—can nowhere be better seen than here. . . ."[1] But in spite of these difficulties, it is possible to obtain, at all events, some traces of the "Heilbringer" conception. From what was said above (p. 68) about the conflict between the sun-god Rā and the dragon Apophis, one would expect, on the Hebrew and Babylonian analogies, that Rā would appear in the character of "Heilbringer"; some slight traces are, indeed, to be found of this. Thus he appears in some of the legends as a man who lived on earth and gave gifts to his people. There is, however, another personality in the Egyptian pantheon, who figures, according to one account at all events, more clearly as a "Heilbringer" proper, namely Osiris: "The Greek version of the myth describes the conduct of Osiris as a 'culture-hero.' He instituted laws, taught agriculture, instructed the Egyptians in the ritual of worship, and won them from 'their destitute and bestial mode of living.' After civilizing Egypt, he travelled over the world. . . ."[2] Later on

[1] *Op. cit.* pp. 132, 133.   [2] Lang, *op. cit.* p. 137.

the same writer says: "The conclusions to be drawn ... are, that in Egypt, as elsewhere, a mythical and a religious, a rational and an irrational stream of thought flowed together, and even to some extent mingled their waters. The rational tendency, declared in prayers and hymns, amplifies the early human belief in a protecting and friendly personal power making for righteousness. The irrational tendency, declared in myth and ritual, retains and elaborates the early human confusions of thought between man and beast and god, things animate and inanimate. . . . Egyptian religion and myth are thus no isolated things; they are but the common stuff of human thought, decorated or distorted under a hundred influences in the course of unknown centuries of years."[1] It is the "rational tendency" of "the early human belief in a protecting and friendly personal power" which points to the idea, in early Egyptian religion, of the "Heilbringer."

Among the *Aryan* races we have a number of instances of "Heilbringers"; a few are referred to here. Indra appears in purely human form. Vritra, too, is represented as an earthly being, half serpent, half man. In the conflict between these two they fight with human weapons; Indra is victorious, and crushes Vritra. In the story of how Indra, assisted by the Angira (the

[1] Lang, *op. cit.* p. 147.

forefathers of the priestly race) gets the cows from the Pani, and gives them to the priests, we have some genuine human *traits*, originally, whatever later meaning may have been attached to the myth; as Breysig says : " Here also it is more probable . . . that an earthly-human legend of the conflict lies behind, which is only a variation of the other ancient accounts of this combat, and instead of the Dragon a number of human enemies appear, to which has been added the new *trait* of the theft of the cows. For such alteration regarding the original form of the conflict with the Dragon the history of Egyptian religion offers also more than one analogy."[1] Again, Matarisvan, the father of the human race, and the Benefactor who brings fire to his people, is another genuine " Heilbringer "-figure.[2]

As regards *Zoroastrian* belief mention should be made of the hero *Shaoshyant* (=" Saviour ") ; this word, according to Böklen (*op. cit.* p. 91), comes from a root meaning " to be of use," " to benefit." He is stated to have been miraculously descended from Zoroaster ; he is to renew the world by purifying it and destroying all evil ; the function of raising the dead at the end of the world is also assigned to him. Although the *Shaoshyant* cannot be said to represent a " Heilbringer "-figure as far as present indications go, it is possible

[1] Breysig, *op. cit.* p. 145.   [2] *Ibid*, p. 146.

THE EVOLUTION OF THE MESSIANIC IDEA

that in an earlier stage of Zoroastrian belief he may have done so ; judging from analogous cases this might be expected. The advanced form in which the Persian religion has been preserved of necessity presupposes a far more primitive form at some earlier period, in which the *Shaoshyant* would have occupied a very different position ; but of that more primitive stage we know nothing. " Positive information regarding the religious condition of Western Iran during the oldest historical period is almost entirely wanting. It is not absolutely certain, for example, of what faith Cyrus the Great was an adherent. With reference, moreover, to the antecedent conditions in Eastern Iran, which must have played an important *rôle* in the early development of the Persian religion, our sources are very scanty throughout." [1] The derivation of the word *Shaoshyant* favours the theory of his having at one time occupied the position of a beneficent hero ; it is for this reason mainly that he is mentioned here.

In *Greek* myth there are, of course, a number of figures to which the term " Heilbringer " could be appropriately applied. Thus Dionysus, during his travels, taught the people of various countries the cultivation of the vine. Prometheus, the great benefactor of men, stole fire from heaven for their benefit ; he taught mortals all the

[1] *Encycl. Bibl.* iv. 5428.

useful arts; according to one legend he created man out of earth and water. Again, the Pythian Apollo, the dragon-slayer, appears in the true character of " Heilbringer "; for besides his victory over the monster, he benefits men in a variety of ways; he teaches them the healing arts; he shows how civil constitutions are formed; and he protects flocks and cattle; as Apollo Musagetes he instructs men in the musical art.

As in the case of the *Tehom*-myth, so here we find that the essential idea of a " Heilbringer " is found in the myths of a very large variety of races in the lower stages of culture. It is not necessary to go into the details of these myths here, as, for the present purpose, it is quite sufficient merely to indicate the way in which the different figures are regarded as " Heilbringers." Among the *Algonquins*, Michabo, the Great Hare, created men out of the carcases of animals; he then taught them all kinds of useful arts, e.g. how to light fires, how to make bows, to construct boats, to make fishing-nets, and snow-shoes; he it was who drove away the cannibals; he lives at the place of the sun-rising.[1] Again, the guardian of the *Iroquois* is Joskeha, who became the father of mankind; " the earth was at first arid and sterile, but Joskeha destroyed

[1] See Schoolcraft, *Algic Researches* (1839); cf. Brinton, *Myths of the New World* passim (1876).

THE EVOLUTION OF THE MESSIANIC IDEA

the gigantic frog which had swallowed all the waters, and guided the torrents into smooth streams and lakes ; [1] he taught men the use of fire, and how to cultivate maize ; he dwells at the extreme edge of the sky, near the sun-rising.[2] Among the *Thlinkeets* the " Heilbringer " appears in the shape of the Crow-man, Yehl "; he is the Benefactor of his race ; he flies over the sea and procures fire for them ; he also brings the sun, moon and stars for his people's benefit ; for their sakes, too, he causes the animals, birds and fishes to come into being. All these things are recounted in a playful, serio-comic manner, but in such a way that, as in other cases of a like kind, it is all evidently looked upon as genuine history. Yehl is always conceived of as a real personality ; he belongs no doubt to prehistoric times, but as the historical consciousness and their ideas of the past among primitive peoples, as a rule, only go back to two or three generations, he is probably thought of as belonging to a time in the not very dim past." [3] Or, again, to take an example from a different centre, South America, the *Bakaïris* venerate a " Heilbringer " called Keri ; he is, as usual, human ; his first act as Benefactor

---

[1] Paul Le Jeune, *Relations de la nouvelle France* (1636), p. 103 ; quoted by Lang, *op. cit.* i, 42.
[2] Brinton, *American Hero-Myths*, pp. 53 ff. (1882).
[3] Breysig, *op. cit.* p. 11.

NAMAQUA AND ZULU "HEILBRINGERS"

was to procure for his people the sun, which he snatched from the red Urubu, the king of eagles; as a result night and day follow each other in a regular course, which had not been possible before, owing to the erratic way in which the eagle had carried the sun about. Keri is a creator, in a modified way, for owing to the fact that there was an insufficient number of Bakaïris, he added to their number by carving them out of pieces of wood. Among the benefits which he gave to his people were fire and water, hammocks, the art of catching fish, and how to cook; he also brought them wool and tobacco.[1] Turning now to a few African examples; among the *Namaquas* there is a semi-divine hero, Heitsi Eibib, who is believed to have been the means of bringing many things into existence, he himself having been born in a miraculous manner; he appears as a Benefactor to his race, among whom he is spoken of as their "great father." The *Zulus* believe that the origin of all things is to be traced to Unkulunkulu, "the old, old one"; he brought men into being by splitting them out of stones, and then imparted to them a knowledge of all things useful. He is, however, a somewhat vague figure, and one whose memory seems to be gradually dying out. "Unkulunkulu is not worshipped, though ancestral spirits are worshipped, because he lived so

[1] Breysig, *op. cit.* pp. 44 ff.

THE EVOLUTION OF THE MESSIANIC IDEA

long ago that no one can now trace his pedigree to the being who is at once the first man and the creator. His ' honour-giving name ' is lost in the lapse of years, and the family rites have become obsolete." [1] The *Bushmen* have an heroic figure in Cagn, who made all things, and to whom prayer is made thus : " O Cagn, O Cagn, are we not your children ? Do you not see our hunger ? Give us food." Cagn had a tooth which was " great medicine," this he lent to people ; he is in some respects very human, thus he has a great collection of charms which he keeps " in his belt." In other respects he has power which is superhuman ; he can change himself, and others, into different animals. " It was formerly said that when men died they went to Cagn, but it has been denied by later Bushmen sceptics." [2] Of more advanced culture are the *Zuñis*—Pueblo Indians of New Mexico and Arizona—they have their culture-hero, Po'shaink'ia, who appears in human form ; he taught men agriculture, after which he left the world. " He is still attentive to prayer. He divided the world up into regions, and gave the animals their homes and functions, much as Heitsi Eibib did in Namaqualand. These animals carry out the designs of the culture-hero, and punish initiated Zuñis who

[1] Lang, *op. cit.* I, 174 ; cf. the same author's work, *The Making of Religion*, pp. 164 ff. (1900).

[2] Lang, *Myth, Ritual and Religion*, II. 36 f.

OTHER INSTANCES OF "HEILBRINGERS"

are careless of their religious duties and ritual."[1] Again, the *Mayas* of Yucatan had a god, Kukulcan, who apparently partook of the nature of a "Heilbringer" in earlier times; he taught his people the art of building; after he had finished his work on earth he went to the land of the setting sun. The people believed that he went to heaven, where he lives in his great house and looks down upon them, and helps and protects those who believe in him.[2] Once more, the *Ahts* of Vancouver's Island have a semi-divine hero, who once dwelt on earth, Quawteaht; his exploits "in the beginning of things were something between those of Zeus and Prometheus ' He is the general framer—I do not say creator—of all things, though some special things are excepted.'. . . In Quawteaht mingle the rough draughts of a god and of an Adam, a creator and a first man."[3]

These instances could likewise be greatly multiplied; but, as will have been noticed, they are taken from peoples widely separated from each other, and thus testify to a similar tendency in belief among very varied races. Throughout we meet with a personality who is semi-divine and semi-human, who is usually a creator, who always

[1] Lang, *Myth, Ritual and Religion*, II. 37.
[2] Breysig, *op. cit.* p. 55.
[3] Lang, *op. cit.* II. 74.

brings blessings to his people, and who is regarded as the help and stay of men. It is true, the characteristic of "Dragon-slayer," or something more or less equivalent, does not always appear, though among the more civilized races this is so ; but in the fragmentary state in which so many of the legends have come down to us, this is scarcely to be wondered at ;[1] in any case, the main thought of a semi-divine benefactor is invariably present.

[1] It is more than probable that in many cases this characteristic never existed, for H. Schmidt truly remarks : " . . . But we also find . . . traditions of the Creation which know nothing of a conflict."—*Jona ; Eine Untersuchung zur vergleichenden Religionsgeschichte*, p. 87 (1907).

CHAPTER X.

THE " PARADISE-MYTH."

One conception underlies all forms of the " Paradise-myth "—Usually it consists of two parts, a past and a future, which did not originally exist together—The supposed steps by which this myth was arrived at—Some Biblical passages considered: Gen. ii. 8–iii.; Ps. xlviii. 2–4; Ezek. xxviii. 13–15; Isa. ii. 2–4 (= Mic. iv. 1–3); Isa. xi. 1–9; Isa. xxxv. 1–10—Inferences to be drawn from these passages.

In the very varied forms in which this myth has been preserved among many peoples there is one underlying idea which is common to all; in each case man is depicted as being in a state of happiness and contentment. According to the theory here advocated this conception arose, in its earliest beginnings, owing to an innate characteristic in man generally, namely, the desire to be happy. Just as the idea of happiness is a relative one, and varies greatly according to the different ideals of men, so the myths which describe these ideals naturally differ very much in form. But all, at bottom, express the same yearning.

Speaking generally, the myth consists of two complementary parts; the one refers to a very early period in the history of man, the other to a time in the distant future. Originally these two cannot have existed together. It lies in the

THE EVOLUTION OF THE MESSIANIC IDEA

nature of things that early man should have been concerned with the present and past before he turned his eyes to the future. If primitive man, in the first instance, framed his ideas upon facts of experience, it was obviously the present that absorbed his attention first; from this the next step would have been to consider what had been; for this either was, or was believed to have been, within the experience of those who had lived before him. It must, that is to say, have been a psychological necessity for man in an early stage of culture to occupy himself with what was and what had been, before that which was going to be.

What the present writer conceives to have been the steps in the natural process whereby the conception of a " Golden Age " was arrived at have already been referred to;[1] but the theory with regard to this may here be briefly stated once more. Given the desire to be happy as an element in man's nature, it will follow of necessity that the desire will in time crystallize into day-dreams; such day-dreams will in course of time assume a more or less definite form, and when communicated to men by each other—which is also a very natural proceeding—a fixed tradition tends to be developed; and such a tradition would inevitably come to be regarded as the echo of something that actually happened some

[1] See pp. 35 f.

long time ago. This step, when once reached, would form a tangible basis upon which to build superstructures, and men would yearn for the happy time that once existed, and by degrees there would be formulated a definite hope that in time to come that happy period would repeat itself; and then, finally, the hope would develop into a fixed expectation.

Whatever other considerations may have entered in and contributed towards the formation of the "Golden Age-" or "Paradise-" myth—and such there must certainly have been—the original and main cause seems to have been due to natural instinct.

* * * * *

The " Paradise-Myth " among the Hebrews.

[Literature: Gressmann, *op. cit.* pp. 193–250—Cheyne, *op. cit.* pp. 71–102.—Dillmann, *op. cit.* pp. 39–84.—Gunkel, *Genesis*, pp. 3–10, 21–36.]

The order in which the following passages are taken is immaterial, because even if considered in (as far as this is possible to determine) chronological order, it would not necessarily mean that the history of the idea of the "Golden Age" in the Old Testament was being treated chronologically; for some of the later books contain remnants of a more ancient form of the myth than some of the earlier ones; or, at all events, more archaic

THE EVOLUTION OF THE MESSIANIC IDEA

traits are sometimes found preserved in some of the later books, e.g. some of the *data* found in *Ezekiel*, *Psalms*, and *Job* show more ancient signs than those contained in *Genesis*. The passages will, therefore, be dealt with in the familiar order of the English Bible.

(*a*) **Genesis ii. 8–iii.** It will not be necessary to deal verse by verse with this passage; one feels the truth of Cheyne's remark (*op. cit.* p. 83), that the story is " very incomplete, and has been manipulated "; so that to deal with it after the manner of a commentary would necessitate the bringing in of many subjects which are unconnected with the present one. Our subject is to indicate certain points in the narrative which have a bearing upon our present investigation.

i. The story presents us with the picture of a beautiful garden in which the first man and the first woman, having all they required, lived happily and contentedly. The scene is thus placed in a period long ago. The restriction to the first man and woman *only* is a later feature. It would appear that some form of the " Golden Age " myth had been utilized by connecting it with the creation story, and then adapting it to the requirements of a later time. The whole narrative is strongly ætiological in character, it gives the answers to many questions upon which

GENESIS II. 8-III.

men must have been speculating.[1] In a more original form, a race of men must have been presupposed, as in the case of the story of Cain and Abel (see Genesis iv. 14-15); that only one man appears must be due to the fact that this story has been brought into connection with the creation story.

ii. Man lives in perfect harmony with the animals; this is a characteristic point of the "Golden Age" myth; wild beasts were a constant source of worry, both on account of their danger to men, and on account of the damage they did to flocks; in the time of peace and happiness, therefore, the "beasts of the field" must have been harmless.

iii. The archaic *traits* with which the narrative abounds show that ancient material was used; this was part of the floating myth–material to which reference has been made in earlier chapters. Such archaic *traits* are, for example, the mention of the Tree of Life, the bringing of the animals to Adam to receive their names, the method of Eve's creation, etc. A further indication of the fact that pre-existing material was being utilized is afforded by the clear marks that more than one tradition underlies the narrative in its present form.[2]

[1] Cf. Gunkel, *Genesis*, p. 25-28.
[2] Cf. on this point Gunkel, *op. cit.* pp. 21-24.

iv. The relationship that exists between man and God ; they converse together, and a certain companionship is represented as existing between them ; above all, man lives in God's "garden." In a more original form of the story it is extremely probable that the garden was not made on purpose for the man, as is implied in ii. 8 ; if, as appears more than probable, the compiler of this narrative was indebted to sources which had, for long, been more or less common property, one can understand the contradiction of, on the one hand, the existence of this companionship, and, on the other, the words : *It is not good that man should be alone.* In the old sources, one surmises that the " garden " must have been occupied by many gods (hence the plural *Elohim*) and many men, for it is certain that early man, with his innate social instincts, would never have pictured to himself either a solitary god or a solitary man ; these are so represented in the present form of the narrative, the one, owing to advanced monotheistic ideas, the other, owing to ætiological considerations, as already pointed out.

v. The garden of Eden is Jahwe-Elohim's " garden " ; when we read in iii. 8 of " Jahwe-Elohim walking in the garden in the cool of the day," the inference is obvious that this was his habit, and that he was enjoying himself on his own domain ; hence we read also of Eden being

GENESIS II. 8-III

"the garden of Elohim" in Ezekiel xxviii. 13, and "the garden of Jahwe" in Genesis xiii. 10; Isaiah li. 3.

vi. In ii. 10 mention is made of the river which "went out of Eden to water the garden"; this river parts into four and waters different lands; the place whence the river issued must, therefore, obviously have been conceived as high up, i.e. on a mountain, "Jahwe's holy mountain" (Isa. ii. 2; Micah iv. 1), "Elohim's mountain" (Ps. xlviii. 2 (1),), "Elohim's holy mountain" (Ezek. xxviii. 14). This mountain is elsewhere spoken of as "in the uttermost parts of the north" (Isa. xiv. 13). Again, we read of there being in the garden "every tree that is pleasant to the sight, and good for food" (ii. 9); mention is made in Ezekiel (xxxi. 8–9) of the beautiful trees that grow in the "garden of Elohim." These are all mythological *traits* which will come before us again presently. The serpent has already been dealt with in an earlier section.

The points enumerated above seem to indicate clearly enough that in the narrative contained in Genesis ii. 8–iii. we have the remains of an ancient myth which has been utilized by a compiler, who adapted it to his special purposes. The myth tells that there was a time, long ago, when man was happy, when he associated with the gods, when he had plenty to eat and drink, when all was

THE EVOLUTION OF THE MESSIANIC IDEA

peaceful, even the animals, and when there was no need to work (cf. iii. 17-19), or at all events when work was pleasanter and more congenial (cf. ii. 15). Moreover, the narrative gives some details, and hints at others, about the locality in which man lived during this happy era; it was in a beautiful garden, the abode of the gods (*Elohim*), where the loveliest trees grew, bearing wonderful fruit, and where a river flowed; and the garden was situated on a mountain. The whole must have presented to the minds of men a fascinating picture of calm and peace and contentment and happiness; and when they contrasted it with the present a great yearning must have possessed them, a longing that that peaceful time might come again.

(*b*) **Psalm xlviii. 2-4 (1-3) :**

Great is Jahwe, and highly to be praised,
In the city of our God, upon His holy mountain ;
Beautiful in elevation (is it), the joy of the whole earth
Is Mount Zion, in the uttermost parts of the north ; the city of the Great King.
God, in her citadels, is known as a tower of refuge.

The text in verse 2 does not seem to be quite in order, and perhaps the reading suggested by

Kittel, and accepted by Briggs, is to be preferred, viz :

> *Great and highly to be praised in the city is our God. . . . .*

This would not, however, affect the significance of the passage as far as the present connexion is concerned. The " city of God " which is situated upon " His holy mountain " is, of course, used appropriately enough of Zion ; but two considerations go to suggest that we have here an adaptation of some earlier material. The words, *Beautiful in elevation, the joy of the whole earth*, reveal an old-world idea of a city placed on so high a mountain that it can be seen far and wide, even over the whole world ; it is the same idea as that contained in Isaiah ii. 2 : *And it shall come to pass in the latter days that the mountain of Jahwe's house shall be established on the top of the mountains, and shall be exalted above all the hills ; and all nations shall flow into it.* Originally there was, of course, no thought of a city or a house ; but the city of Jerusalem and the Temple were, by a very natural development, represented as situated within what was in the first instance only the garden of God ; as we have seen, this garden was conceived of as situated on a mountain. But still more significant are the words which follow, for they speak of the mountain as being " in

the uttermost parts of the north "; these words require a little examination. *Yar^ekāh* (="uttermost parts") has, almost invariably, the idea of distance underlying its use; in Genesis xlix. 13, where the word is translated "border" in the R.V., it is used poetically for expressing the more distant border of Zebulon's territory;[1] in the same way, of the extreme hinder part of the tabernacle (Exod. xxvi. 22, etc.), the innermost recesses of a cave (1 Sam. xxiv. 14), the innermost parts of a house (Amos. vi. 10), etc. The R.V. rendering, therefore, " on the sides of the north " does not commend itself, nor does that of Briggs—
" the northern ridge "—who explains it by saying
". . . the temple being on the north-eastern corner or back of Mount Zion, looked at from the south,"[2] for neither satisfy the idea of extreme distance in connexion with the north that the phrase seems to demand; indeed, it is interesting to find that in Isaiah xiv. 13; Ezekiel xxxviii. 6, 15; xxxix. 2, where the identical phrase occurs, the R.V. renders it " in the uttermost parts of the north." The translation given above may, then, be regarded as justifiable. But this " furthest north " is elsewhere pointed to as heaven, a place situated upon a mount, which reaches above the clouds : *And thou saidst in thine*

[1] Cf. Oxford Hebrew Lexicon, s.v.
[2] *Psalms* (International Critical Commentary) i. 410.

EZEKIEL XXVIII. 13-15

heart, I will ascend into heaven, I will exalt my throne above the stars of God ; I will sit upon the mount of congregation, in the uttermost part of the north : I will ascend above the heights of the clouds ; I will be like the Most High. (Isa. xiv. 13, 14). And this abode of God in the furthest north corresponds with what is said in Genesis ii. 14–15, according to which the garden of Eden was located in the north.[1] In the same way the "four living creatures," who came from the abode of Jahwe, appeared from out of a great cloud which "*came from the north*" (Ezek. i. 4) ; and again, those that are bidden to come to Jahwe "*came from the way of the upper gate, which lieth toward the north*. . . ." In the north, therefore, Jahwe's abode was believed to be. This point has been emphasized because, as will be seen in the next chapter, it corresponds with what was believed to be the abode of the gods according to other forms of the "Golden Age" myth.

The passage (Ps. xlviii. 2-4) which we have been considering, therefore, contains some archaic elements which refer to the abode of Jahwe, where, in ages long ago, man dwelt in peace and contentment.

(c) **Ezekiel xxviii. 13–15.** *In Eden, the garden of God, wast thou ; with all manner of costly stones wast*

[1] Cf. too, Genesis ii. 11 : ". . . *Where there is gold*," with Job xxxvii. 22 : "*Out of the north cometh gold.*"

thou covered : ruby, carnelian and diamond, topaz, onyx and jasper, sapphire, carbuncle and emerald ; and thy garment (?) and thy settings (?) were of wrought gold in the day that thou wast created. I had determined that thou shouldst be a companion of the Cherubim ; thou wast upon the mountain of God ; thou didst walk among the fiery stones. Perfect wast thou from the day that thou wast created, until unrighteousness was found in thee.[1]

These words, spoken in reference to the King of Tyre, only become comprehensible when it is realized that they contain elements of an ancient myth which has been utilized for the purpose of depicting the downfall of the King of Tyre in the most impressive way. These elements are taken from the " Paradise-myth," i.e., the Hebrew form of the " Golden Age " myth. At one time, long ago, man lived in the most glorious estate in Eden, Jahwe's garden, situated on the mountain of God ; there he abode until, through his own folly, he was driven out, and was no longer permitted to be a companion of the gods. This is all taken and used in reference to the King of Tyre. But the way in which these elements are brought in shows that the prophet was using myth-material that was current, and familiar to his hearers. The myth

[1] This is Cornill's rendering ; for the text-critical notes which justify the above see his *Das Buch des Propheten Ezechiel*, pp. 360 ff. (1886).

as it appears here is a variant of the Genesis form ; but the main points, especially for our present purpose, are the same, viz. there was a time when man lived in contentment, in companionship with the gods.

The passages so far touched upon contain re-echoes of the past ; there are others in which the ideas dealt with are likewise based upon the past (or, more strictly speaking, what was believed to have happened in the past), but they are used for constructing pictures of the *future*.

(*d*) **Isaiah ii. 2–4 (= Micah iv. 1–3).** This passage is more fully dealt with below. Here it is the last verse of the passage which claims a passing notice. It speaks of a time when there shall be universal peace, and all warlike weapons shall be done away with : *They shall beat their swords into plowshares and their spears into pruning hooks : nation shall not lift up sword against nation, neither shall they learn war any more.* This idea seems to owe its origin to the " Golden Age " myth, for there a similar *trait* is found ; it was a time of universal peace, for men dwelt in Jahwe's garden (according to the Hebrew form of the myth) where everything was peaceful, and there was therefore no need for weapons. According to a later tradition the use of weapons was taught by Azazel, or Azael according to the form which occurs in the following passage :

THE EVOLUTION OF THE MESSIANIC IDEA

" Azael, the tenth of the rulers, first taught (men) to make swords and shields and every weapon of war " (*Enoch* viii. 1).[1] In other forms of the " Golden Age " myth, to be referred to in the next chapter, the absence of weapons is likewise a characteristic. It is, therefore, probable that in the passage before us the prophet was utilizing material which had long been floating among the people, and depicted the Age that he looked for in terms of that of which men had often heard.

(*e*) **Isaiah xi. 1-9.** This passage will, likewise, have to be dealt with in a later chapter ; here the verses that specially concern us are 6-9. In these there is presented a picture of the conditions of things as they existed on Jahwe's holy mountain long ago ; and these conditions are again transferred from the distant past to the future. The points of correspondence between this passage and the account of the garden of Eden in Genesis ii. 8 ff. may be briefly indicated. The ruler referred to in Isaiah xi. 1-5, who is to judge with righteousness, corresponds to Jahwe, who is supreme in Paradise ; the unity that the Isaianic passage describes as existing among the animals, is paralleled by the Genesis account of how all the animals were brought to the man to be named ; in the former the mention of the child leading them enhances

[1] *The Book of Enoch* . . . ed. R. H. Charles, p. 65 (1893).

ISAIAH XI. 1-9

the picture of peace, and also presents a substitute for Adam; Isaiah xi. 9 reveals where this reign of peace is to be—it is on Jahwe's " holy mountain " ; as we have seen, according to Genesis ii. 10 ff., the garden of Eden was situated on a mountain ; and in the same verse in Isaiah the mention of the " knowledge of Jahwe " recalls the " tree of knowledge of good and evil " in Genesis ii. 17, however different the fundamental ideas in either passage may be. We have already seen some reason for regarding the narrative in Genesis ii. 8 ff. as being based on myth-material which had been current among the people ; the same must be the case here if, as seems incontestable, an organic unity underlies the two accounts ; in the present case, indeed, other grounds as well can be advanced for thinking that Isaiah is only adapting, not originating, the picture before us ; in the words of Gunkel : " This description may not be regarded as an invention of the prophet. If it were that it would be extraordinarily phantastic, and in the mouth of a man like Isaiah almost incomprehensible. Its meaning only becomes clear when it is recognized that the prophet is utilizing for his own purposes material which had been handed down by tradition. He is citing here the well-known myth of the Golden Age." [1] On comparing the regular Isaianic passages—

[1] *Chaos und Schöpfung*, p. 13.

THE EVOLUTION OF THE MESSIANIC IDEA

which contain the prophet's distinctive thoughts and language, etc., one realizes how extremely improbable it is that Isaiah should have formed the ideas contained in these verses. He takes the old myth, which was familiar to the people, and adapts it to his Messianic teaching. We shall refer to this again.

(*f*) **Isaiah xxxv. 1-10.** There are a few points in this chapter which show that the idea of the " Golden Age " lay at the back of the writer's mind. The transformation of the wilderness into a place of beauty and joy, where there shall be seen " the glory of Jahwe and the excellency of our God," recalls the thought of Jahwe's beautiful garden. The chapter continues to speak of the time when sickness shall cease—the lame man leaping, the blind seeing, the deaf hearing, the dumb breaking forth into song ; further, there is to be " the way of holiness," upon which only the good may pass ; no wild beasts shall be there to harm men ; there will be " joy and gladness " ; and " sorrow and sighing shall flee away." There are here some of the characteristic signs of the " Golden Age "—peace, contentment, and happiness. Again the prophet is using well-known material, and adapting it to his Messianic teaching. The mention of Zion in verse 10 suggests another passage, Isaiah li. 3, in which it is said that Jahwe has comforted the waste places

ISAIAH XXXV. 1-10

of Zion, *and hath made her wilderness like Eden and her desert like the garden of Jahwe*; and, further, it says that there will be joy and gladness and singing. Here again, it is impossible to resist the conviction that the prophet is utilizing current material. The transference of the original " mountain of God " from the mythic garden of Eden to mount Zion was easy and natural.[1]

These passages, then, (and they could easily be added to,) point to the fact that the myth of the " Golden Age " was well known to the Israelites, and that some of their teachers made use of this material, and adapted it to Messianic prophecy.

[1] In another set of conceptions God's abode on mount Horeb was conceived of as having been transferred to mount Zion.

CHAPTER XI.

THE "PARADISE-MYTH" AMONG OTHER PEOPLES.

THE *raison d'être* of this myth probably varied in different ages, but the main and original idea which gave birth to it remained constant all through—Different forms of the myth considered: Babylonian, Phœnician, Arab, Egyptian, Zoroastrian, Greek, Roman, Algonquin, Sioux, Gallas, Akwapim—These, again, are only a few examples of a great number.

[LITERATURE : See references in the footnotes.]

"MYTHS of a Golden Age, long since passed away, in which gods and men lived in closer union, and happiness and justice prevailed on earth, formed the background of most, if not all, heathen religious systems."[1] The truth of this statement may be illustrated by a few typical examples. The existence of the myth, though it be in greatly varying form, in so many widely separated centres will, as in the case of the myths already referred to, afford some justification for the belief that when the Hebrew teachers used a similar myth and adapted it to higher teaching, they were utilizing material which, in its fundamentals, was practically the common property of the world. In an earlier chapter the origin of the idea of the "Golden Age" (or "Paradise," according to the Hebrew form) was stated to have

[1] Wordsworth, *The One Religion* (1881).

THE GOLDEN AGE

been due to the innate desire of man to be happy, a desire which present stress must have constantly tended to strengthen. As feelings of this kind were common to man, and as these feelings would inevitably be expressed in tangible form, there is no reason for assuming one original form of the " Golden Age " myth—it pressed itself to the fore all the world over, originally; so that the Hebrews inherited from their forefathers traditional matter which these had shared with the world in general. Every age expresses itself differently, and as time proceeded, the *raison d'être* of the belief in the " Golden Age " must have varied, though, at bottom, the original idea still held sway; but as new elements entered into the daily life of man, and changes took place in his environment, his mental attitude towards the ancient beliefs naturally varied; in some respects an advancing civilization only intensified his longing for the time of happiness long ago. So that the theory here held as to an elemental characteristic in man being the earliest and original cause of a " Golden Age " myth, in its primeval form, only receives confirmation from Dillmann's very luminous words as to the thought-connexion in the minds of the Hebrew thinkers when they formulated upon the basis of earlier material—" undoubtedly similar conceptions were held already among the earlier Hebrews "—

the specifically Hebrew type of the myth: "When one examines the thought-connexion of the story (i.e. the Paradise story in *Genesis*) it is seen that the starting-point lies in the enigmatical fact that man, although standing in relationship to God, and capable of striving for that which is highest, and ever making progress in conquering and impressing his power upon all things outside of himself, is, in spite of all this, subject to unnumbered sufferings, evils, and hardships; and, more especially, that although filled with an ineradicable yearning for permanent happiness, he yet never reaches this goal, but, on the contrary, succumbs, like all other earthly beings, to death and corruption. The contradiction which is seen to exist here has from of old led men to the conviction that things cannot originally have been so. It was, moreover, easy to see that these evils had tended to increase rather than decrease with the march of history, and that men were happier in the earlier, simpler conditions of life. Hence it has come about that among all races a belief in a happier time long ago has been formulated, differing in form according to the genius of each race."[1]

Although, as far as is known, the *Babylonians* have not preserved any definite form of the "Golden Age" myth, there are various indications

[1] *Op. cit.* p. 43.

THE BABYLONIAN MYTH

that something more or less parallel did exist among them. Jeremias draws attention to the fact that an ancient name of Babylon, *Tin. Ter (Ki)*, "The abode of life," points to the name Bab-ilu as meaning " The gate of God," and that therefore this meaning, which popular etymology had already assigned to it, is correct. It is perhaps in reference to Babylon that an ancient epic speaks of the holy mount of cedars, the " abode of the gods," where the Elamitic Hero Humbaba " with stately step walks upon the well-cultivated path."[1]

Other references are found to a garden of the gods, into which men seem to have entrance, Gilgamesh and Eabani are mentioned besides Humbaba; it is true these are all great heroes, but they are differentiated from the gods (cf. Adam and Jahwe). In this garden, which is situated on a mountain, there are holy trees with delicious fruit; and there is a river with the water of life.[2] In the *Book of Enoch* (ch. xxv.) there is a striking passage which recalls what has just been said : " 3. And he answered me and said, ' This high mountain which thou hast seen, whose summit is like the throne of the Lord, is His

[1] Jeremias, *op. cit.* p. 93.

[2] For further details see Jeremias, *op. cit.* pp. 92–104. Cf. Lenormant, *op. cit.* I. 74 ff.; Baudissin, *Studien* II. 189 f. Dillmann, *op. cit.* pp. 48 f.; cf. Jeremias, *op. cit.* pp. 112 f., 121 ff.

throne, where the Holy and Great One, the Lord of Glory, the Eternal King, will sit when He shall come down to visit the earth with goodness. 4. And no mortal is permitted to touch this tree of delicious fragrance till the great day of judgment, when He shall avenge and bring everything to its consummation for ever; this tree, I say, will then be given to the righteous and humble. 5. By its fruit life will be given to the elect: it will be transplanted to the north, to the holy place, to the temple of the Lord, the Eternal King. 6. Then will they rejoice with joy and be glad: they will enter the holy habitation: the fragrance thereof will be in their limbs, and they will have a long life on earth, such as thy fathers have lived: and in their days no sorrow or pain or trouble or calamity will affect them " (xxv. 3–6).[1] It is clear that there are points of affinity between this passage and what was said about Babylonian belief; but still clearer is it that in this *Enoch* passage the writer is using a form of the " Golden Age " myth and adapting it, by transplanting it to the future; the sixth verse makes this quite unmistakeable.

The Babylonian belief, moreover, concerning the abode of the Blessed in the next world seems also to echo some early form of a " Golden Age " myth. Hommel, in touching on this subject,

[1] Charles, *op. cit.* pp. 98, 99; cf. lxxvii. 3.

THE BABYLONIAN MYTH

says : " The purely mythological conception of the Babylonians . . . which takes us down into the nethermost depths of the earth as the abode not only of the dead, but also of the Blessed departed, merits some more detailed consideration. . . . I have already drawn attention to the fact that one of the Babylonian names for the nether-world was *Arallu*, and that this very name was, in ancient times, borrowed by the Egyptians in the form of *Ijalu*, but that it was used as a name for the abode of the Blessed. . . . The Babylonians, however, did not only call Hades *Arallu*; but the great ' World-mountain,' upon which the heavenly gods are enthroned, and upon which they have been born from all eternity, this too was called *Arallu*. This same mountain was also regarded by them as the ' Golden Mount,' and its locality was in the furthest north. . . . And that the pious sufferer Job (xxxvii. 22) refers to the same mythical mount of the gods is clear when we read his words in the light of what has been said. It is there written : *Out of the north comes the gold, God hath upon Him terrible majesty* (splendour) ; or, in other words, ' Upon the golden mount, in the uttermost parts of the north, dwells God, and upon this mount is His unapproachable majesty enthroned. . . .' Of this there can be no doubt, that the various mountains of the gods among the ancients, above all, Olympus of the Greeks,

THE EVOLUTION OF THE MESSIANIC IDEA

then Ezekiel's holy mount of Paradise, also Meru of the Indians, and others—one and all go back to the conception of the Babylonians concerning the abode of the gods in the furthest north." [1]

Whether the *Phœnicians* preserved their version of the " Golden Age " myth in written form or not cannot be said with certainty, and therefore we are in the dark concerning it ; but in view of the great similarity of religious thought which exists in other respects between the Phœnicians and other northern Semites, it must have had elements in common with Babylonian and Israelite conceptions. On this similarity of belief Pietschmann says of the Phœnicians : " . . . On the other hand, the religion of the Phœnicians and of the other Canaanites rests apparently, in the last instance, upon one and the same historical foundation. It was developed out of a number of religious beliefs and customs which the Canaanites must have brought with them when they entered into what afterwards became their permanent place of settlement. For they share their religion, in all fundamental points, with most of the north Semitic races. . . . Originally it probably had great resemblance to the belief of the Arabs as this existed prior to the rise of Mohammedanism." [2]

[1] *Die Insel der Seligen in Mythus und Sage der Vorzeit*, pp. 35-40 (1901).
[2] *Geschichte der Phönizier*, pp. 155 f. (1869) ; see further pp. 170-191.

PRE-ISLAMIC BELIEF

Unfortunately we know nothing for certain as to whether or not the *Arabs* had a form of the " Golden Age " myth ; there are, it is true, indications in their religion and customs which force the conviction that something of the kind existed ; their conceptions of Paradise, their beliefs (pre-Islamic) as to the nature of their gods, and the character of their feasts, each in their way, suggest the idea that at some time or other something corresponding to the " Golden Age " myth must have existed among them. Pre-Islamic belief concerning their gods shows that the Arabs believed in a close connexion between men and gods : " The heavenly gods are always localized in definite sites on earth. The universality of this fact of localization is very remarkable ; it is explained by the fact of an originally earthly, not a heavenly, nature of the gods." [1] This earthly nature of the gods brings them nearer to men ; though this fact itself does not mean anything as far as the present subject is concerned, it is nevertheless one of the conditions of the existence of the " Golden Age " myth. What, however, is most suggestive, among the Arabs, of the echo of such a myth is the nature of the annual pilgrimages and festivals ; to quote Wellhausen again : " Noticeable are the

[1] Wellhausen, *Reste Arabischen Heidentums*, p. 211 (1897).

THE EVOLUTION OF THE MESSIANIC IDEA

pilgrimages, of the most varied Arab clans, to certain sanctuaries, which exercise an universal power of attraction. Religion (i.e. among the Arabs) has lost its ethical character more and more, and has assimilated to itself a syncretistic form. Owing to this it has been productive of widespread blessings. Amidst the tumult and confusion of the desert, the festivals, at the commencement of each half-year, offer the only pleasing time of peacefulness. A God's-truce, of not short duration, interrupts then the eternal feuds. The most varying tribes, who ordinarily would not trust each other even in crossing a path, make their pilgrimages without fear, traversing the districts of friend or foe, journeying on in company to the same holy spot. Trade becomes possible, and a lively, general intercourse supervenes. One breathes freely, and for a time, at all events, one is relieved of the restraints which usually cause each tribe to segregate itself and keep apart from others. . . . The places in which the festivals are celebrated become fairs and markets; Ukâtz serves as a kind of general meeting-place for all Arabia. . . . This development has, it is true, to some extent resulted in a loss of the religious element. There was not much thought of the fact that the holy months were intended to be devoted to the purposes of worship. . . . The fair in Ukâtz had

THE EGYPTIAN MYTH

a decidedly mundane appearance . . . men gave themselves up to amusement and merriment, to the society of women, to drinking and singing; even Jews and Christians were not excluded from taking part in both trade and amusement." [1] Religious dances played, of course, a leading part in the festivities. Improbable as any connexion between these things and the "Golden Age" myth appears, the possibility of such being the case is not excluded when one recalls some characteristics of certain Greek and Roman feasts which will be referred to presently.

Among the *Egyptians* the *data* concerning a "Golden Age" are quite definite; to quote Maspero (in Pietschmann's translation): ". . . In later times the Egyptians regarded the rule of these divine kings as a Golden Age, of which they never thought without yearning for it, and when it was desired to express something which was delightful beyond imagination, one would say, 'The like was never seen since the days of King Râ.'" [2] The names of the divine kings referred to are given in their Greek form as: Hephaestos, Helios, Zôs, Kronos, Osiris (Onnophris), Typhon, and Horos.

[1] *Op. cit.* pp. 216, 220.

[2] Maspero, *Geschichte der Morgenländischen Völker im Alterthum*, übersetzt von R. Pietschmann, pp. 36 ff. (1877).

THE EVOLUTION OF THE MESSIANIC IDEA

In *Zoroastrian* belief there are striking parallels with the Biblical Paradise and Fall stories; but among the Persians the idea of the " Golden Age " appears more clearly expressed. In speaking of Yima and of the happy age in which he lived, Lenormant says: ". . . Later on he was only the first king of the Iranians, but a king whose life, like that of his subjects, was lived in the midst of the joys of Eden, in the Paradise of Airyana-Vaedja, the abode of primeval man. . . ." [1] In later times the period of the life of bliss was said to have lasted a thousand years, and it was only because of Yima's sin that men forfeited their happy state.[2] In the same way, a " Golden Age " is believed in by the Brahmins, and a detailed account of it is given in the third book of the *Mahabharata*, vv. 11234 ff., of which a short extract may be given—the translation is that of Roth: " Krita, my beloved, is the Age in which Justice is uninterrupted; ' Action ' (Krita), not ' Thou oughtest to act,' is the characteristic of this, the most excellent, Age. The decisions of Justice hold sway, no creatures perish; therefore in later days the Age of Krita was acknowledged as the most perfect. . . . During this Age there was no illness, no deterioration of the senses—no anger, no unhappiness, no

[1] *Les origines* . . . I. 68 ff.
[2] See further *Bund.* xvii., xxiii., xxxii. ; *Yesht* xvii.

GREEK MYTHS

cheating, no hatred; neither was there strife, nor fatigue, nor enmity, nor malice, nor fear, nor pain, nor envy, nor jealousy. Therefore was the highest Brahmin the highest goal of the wise, and the souls of all the beings of Narajana were enlightened. The Brahmana, Kshatrija, Vaiçja, and Çudra, differentiated indeed by their special characteristics, lived together in the Age of Krita, each peacefully occupied in his avocation." It then goes on to say how that during the succeeding ages righteousness decreased, and sorrow and travail of every kind increased.[1]

Among *classical writers* there are some famous passages which must be referred to here. The following from Hesiod's *Works and Days* (ll. 109–120) is one of the best known:

" First of all did the eternal gods, dwellers in Olympian mansions, create a golden race of speech-endowed mortals. They lived in Kronos' days when he reigned in heaven, and they lived as gods, the heart free from care; neither troubles nor sorrows had they, enfeebled old age crossed not their path, but always the same in feet and hands, they delighted themselves in feastings apart from all ills. But they died as though subdued by sleep; and all good things were

[1] R. Roth, *Abhandlung über den Mythus . . . und die Indische Lehre von den vier Weltaltern*, pp. 21 ff. (1860). Cf. Rig-Veda i. 179, 2; vii. 76, 4.

THE EVOLUTION OF THE MESSIANIC IDEA

theirs; and the bounteous earth of her own will nurtured them well and plentifully. And of their own free will peacefully they tilled their lands with many blessings in store." [1]

Cf. also lines 90–93:

"For there lived in earliest times on earth a race of men free from care and trouble, free from wearisome worry, free from painful sickness too, that brings death to men. For mortal men soon age when sorrows hold sway."

The festival of "Kronia" was held at Olympia and Athens; these appear to be the only two places, hitherto known of, on Greek soil at which the worship of Kronos was practised.[2] Mommsen believes the feast of *Kronia* to be, relatively, late in date, and sees in it the desire to represent the time of innocence in a dramatic form at a feast;[3] Frazer, on the other hand, speaks of the (Olympian) *Kronia* as "probably one of the oldest of Greek festivals."[4] Preller says: "According to a tradition which is perhaps to be traced to Philochoros, the month Hekatombaion, in which the feast of *Kronia* falls, was in the time of Theseus called 'Kronion' or Kronios."[5] He

[1] Ed. Flach (1885); see, too, Homer's *Od.* iv. 561–568.
[2] *Pausanias*, I. 18, 7 (ed. Frazer).
[3] *Heortologie. Antiquarische Untersuchungen über die städtischen Feste der Athener*, pp. 79 ff. (1864).
[4] *The Golden Bough* (2nd ed.) III. 149 (1900).
[5] *Griechische Mythologie* (4th ed.) I. 52 (1894).

believes that, upon the whole, external proofs point to the fact that Kronos was taken over from foreign cults, rather than that he is the expression of an ancient Greek idea; indeed the fact seems scarcely to admit of doubt.[1] The feast of *Kronia* was held in midsummer (on the twelfth of Hekatombaion); it was a feast of merriment and general rejoicing, and was regarded as symbolical of the " Golden Age," when all men were equal, and there was peace, plenty and enjoyment on earth. Kronos was king then, and reigned on earth (the " in heaven " in Hesiod, quoted above, is a later idea). Masters and slaves sat down together at this feast, which was intended to recall the time when all men were equal; whether any one represented Kronos cannot be stated with certainty, but the high probability is that this was so.[2] At any rate the *Kronia* undoubtedly was a representation of the conditions that were believed to have obtained in the " Golden Age."

Another important reference is found in Porphyry, *De Abstinentia* iv. 2:

". . . Among those, therefore, who have succinctly and accurately compiled the history of the Greeks, is the Peripatetic Dichæarchus. This

---

[1] See Roscher, *Lexikon der griechischen und römischen Mythologie*, II. 1458.

[2] Frazer, *op. cit.* III. 149.

man, in describing the life of ancient Greece, says that the ancients, being like the gods, and being good by nature and living a perfect life, were considered as a golden race. He compared them to the men of the present age, being as they are of a debased and degraded composition—no living animal was slain. This the poets, too, put before us, and name this race the Golden race, and say :

"'All good things were theirs, and the fruitful earth did of itself bear fruit in great abundance, while they of their own free will tilled their fields in peace with many blessings.'

"In explaining this Dichæarchus says that life in the time of Kronos was of this nature, if one is to take him as a historical and not a legendary figure, to reject the mythical element, and to treat the story in a rational way. That everything grew of its own accord is quite likely, for men certainly did nothing of themselves, for the reason that they did not yet possess either the agricultural nor indeed any other art. The same thing was also the cause of their leading an existence of leisure without labour and care ; and, if one may agree with the conviction of the most accomplished physicians, this was also the cause of their immunity from sickness. . . . But besides this there were neither wars nor factions among them, for there was no prize to be gained which would offer enough incentive for beginning

"SATURNALIA"

such hostilities. So that the sum of their life was mere leisure, rest from the stress of life, health, peace and friendship."

Turning now to Italy, the belief in the existence of a "Golden Age" in the distant past was witnessed to by the annual festival of *Saturnalia*.[1] "This famous festival fell in December, the last month of the Roman year, and was popularly supposed to commemorate the merry reign of Saturn, the god of sowing and of husbandry, who lived on earth long ago as a righteous and beneficent king of Italy, drew the rude and scattered dwellers on the mountains together, taught them to till the ground, gave them laws, and ruled in peace. His reign was the fabled Golden Age; the earth brought forth abundantly; no sound of war or discord troubled the happy world; no baleful love of lucre worked like poison in the blood of the industrious and contented peasantry. Slavery and private property were alike unknown; all men had all things in common. At last the good god, the kindly king, vanished suddenly; but his memory was cherished to distant ages, shrines were reared in his honour, and many hills and high places in Italy bore his name."[2] The organic connexion between the *Kronia* and the

---

[1] For the belief in its return at some future time, cf. Virgil, *Eclog.* iv. ll. 4-6, *Aen.* viii. 319-321.

[2] Frazer, *op. cit.* III. 138. Cf. Preller, *Römische Mythologie*, (3rd ed.) II. 10 ff.

Saturnalia is clear upon the face of it ; etymologically, too, the two names point to the same thing—Kronos being derived from *kraino*, in the sense of " to ripen," and Saturn being akin to *satus* and *satio*, " sowing." The testimony, e.g. of Accius as quoted by Macrobius, is to the same effect : " Maxima pars Graium Saturno et maxime Athenea conficiunt sacra, quae Cronia esse iterantur ab illis." [1]

Finally, just a few references may be given to some echoes of an idea of a " Golden Age " among less civilized races. Many of the legends current among the North American Indians relate how, long ago, the Great Spirit associated with men ; they point to the locality which was the scene of this happy time, a common sanctuary among the *Algonquins* and *Sioux*, called the " Pipe-quarry." Later on, the legend, in some of its forms, tells of how the Great Spirit left men because they were no more obedient to him. The footprints which he left on the rocky ground are still pointed out, they look like those of a great bird ; the Great Spirit is usually, among these people, conceived of as a gigantic bird.[2] Among the *Gallas* of north-east Africa we have perhaps the echo of a kindred idea ; they pray to their

[1] *Sat.* I. 7, 37.
[2] Waitz, *Anthropologie der Naturvölker* III. 179 (1860) ; Schoolcraft, *Algic Researches* III. 233.

AMERICAN AND AFRICAN MYTHS

great god Wake in the following way : " O Wake, take us to thee ; lead us to the garden " (i.e. the garden of Wake).[1] Once more, the *Akwapim*, an east African tribe, tell in their folk-tales how that in earlier times there were purer conceptions of their deity. According to these legends, heaven at that time was nearer to men than now ; the highest god, who was the creator, himself gave words of wisdom to men in those times ; but later on he withdrew himself from men, and now he lives far away in the distant heavens.[2]

Further search would undoubtedly reveal many analogous legends. In all the beliefs referred to above it is impossible not to see the common underlying idea ; this, for our present purpose, is the main point.

[1] Isenberg and Krapf, *Journals . . . describing their proceedings in the kingdom of Shoa . . .*, p. 151 (1843).
[2] Waitz, *op. cit.* II. 171.

PART II.

Some Examples of Adaptation and Development.

PART II.

SOME EXAMPLES OF ADAPTATION AND DEVELOPMENT.

CHAPTER XII.

SUMMARY OF THE MATERIAL DEALT WITH.

The contents of the foregoing chapters summarized, and the salient points emphasized—Attempt to show that in the three myths considered above a logical sequence is discernible—With the later development of these myths this thought-sequence tended to become obscured, and an intermixture between them gradually arose—Signs of this process probably to be seen in some Old Testament passages—Links in the history of the development of ideas become lost in transmission—These facts must be allowed for in studying the adaptation and development of the three myths under consideration.

I.

THE MAIN POINTS ENUMERATED.

BEFORE examining some of the Old Testament passages in which the floating myth-material, to which reference has been made in the preceding chapters, has been utilized and adapted to more spiritual teaching, it will be well to gather up and summarize the various threads of the argument, in order that the different points of attachment

THE EVOLUTION OF THE MESSIANIC IDEA

between the myth-material and the Messianic teaching based upon it may be clearly set forth.

The attempt has been made, in the first place, to show that there is a reasonable probability for believing that some of the earliest forms of myth were, in their origin, the expression of emotions which are innate in human nature. That other elements arose in due time and contributed their *quota* to the development and elaboration of myths lies, of course, in the nature of things; but the original motive-power for the construction of myths must have come from within. When man had once reached that stage of mental evolution in which his ideas, feelings, yearnings and aspirations became capable of taking formal shape, it would not have been long before the primeval poets and prophets gave expression, in one form or another, to that which was surging inarticulate in the hearts of men at large. Each generation produces its representatives to whom, in greater or less degree, the great poet-philosopher's words apply :

Vom frischen Geiste fühl' ich mich durchdrungen ;
Gestalten gross, gross die Erinnerungen !

Among those emotions and yearnings which are common to man's nature three were chosen out as being appropriate to the purpose in hand, viz. the elemental characteristics of fear, the sense of dependence, and the desire to be happy.

SUMMARY OF THE MATERIAL DEALT WITH

It was shown next that there is some justification for believing that the myths whereby these three elemental characteristics in man were expressed were primeval forms of those which in their highly-developed Old Testament guise may be designated the *Tehom-myth*, the *Jahwe-myth*, and the *Paradise-myth*. The existence of these myths, in varying form, among many peoples in very different stages of culture, and widely separated geographically, led to the reasonable supposition that the underlying ideas to which each gave expression were common to man, and that therefore one original form of myth in each case was not to be thought of; though within a given area one original form had doubtlessly been the parent of daughter-myths—this, however, belonged to a later stage in its history altogether. This wide diffusion led to the further supposition that when traces of the three myths in question were found in the Old Testament, the writers were making use of material which had been floating for millenniums; the study of some Old Testament passages made this supposition practically certain, for the very antique *traits* and *naïve* conceptions with which such passages abound proved that very ancient material was being used; moreover, the fact that these ancient elements are really out of place in many cases, and are alien to the spirit of the contexts, and in some

THE EVOLUTION OF THE MESSIANIC IDEA

cases are meaningless unless their antique character is recognized,—all this goes to establish the fact that the Old Testament writers were making use of well-known, pre-existing material, which they adapted to higher teaching. The important point was also laid stress upon that as this myth-material, of hoary antiquity, belonged to the traditions of the people, and had been handed down for untold generations, it must have been regarded with great veneration, and looked upon as a sacred heritage. It is only on this supposition that we can understand how they found any place at all in the Bible. Further, as in later generations more and more spiritual beliefs obtained, many of the ancient elements just referred to must have appeared offensive to the teachers of the people, and to those who were the " Keepers of Holy Writ " ; it was therefore a sacred duty among these to modify as far as possible those passages in which these unwelcome elements were manifest. But the lapse of years had, as was natural enough, brought with it forgetfulness of the real meaning of many of the references to early myth in the passages under consideration ; therefore there was no reason to delete them, and the expurgators were content to leave them, though probably they did not understand them, or else they put a meaning upon them adapted to the more spiritual beliefs of the times. This accounts

SUMMARY OF THE MATERIAL DEALT WITH

for their presence in the text as we now have it.

Examples of the remnants of such pre-existing myth-material in the case of each of the three myths referred to were then given and considered ; likewise examples of other forms of the myths among very various peoples. In each instance it was pointed out that there was no attempt to make these exhaustive, and that they could without difficulty be greatly multiplied ; but the typical examples given were deemed to be sufficient for the purpose in hand.

The salient points in these examples of the remnants of pre-existing myth-material, in so far as they constitute antecedents of the Messianic Idea, may be summarized as follows :

Tehom, the primeval watery monster, is the enemy of the gods and of men ; in the various developments of the myth which, in process of time, must have arisen, *Tehom* comes to be known under a variety of names, viz. the " Serpent," the " Dragon," " Leviathan," and " Rahab " ; and moreover, *Tehom* is identified with the " Sea " ; further, the name *Tehom Rabbah* was probably given in order to differentiate *Tehom* from the brood of *Tanninim* or " dragons." In the great primeval conflict between *Tehom* and the champion of the gods, the former is indeed overcome, but not finally annihilated. Whenever, in the

THE EVOLUTION OF THE MESSIANIC IDEA

Old Testament, this myth is referred to, the writer takes for granted that what he is writing about is matter of common knowledge; the fact becomes entirely intelligible when it is realized that the myth existed in varied form among the most different and widely separated peoples all the world over. It was, furthermore, noticed that, in all probability, two other Old Testament stories are to be regarded as "extensions" of the *Tehom*-myth; thus, in the story of the Fall, the Serpent, who is identified with *Tehom*, appears as the embodiment of the principle of evil; and in the story of the Flood, *Tehom Rabbah* once more appears as the enemy of God.

In the *Jahwe-myth* the chief points are that Jahwe takes the place of the Conqueror of *Tehom*, the arch-enemy; Jahwe is also the Bringer of Blessings to His people. It is important to remember that these actions are *imputed* to Jahwe by the Biblical writers; originally this cannot have been so, but the earlier conceptions concerning a semi-divine hero who overcame the Dragon, and brought blessings to his people, are *transferred* to Jahwe; hence, in part, the reason why, not infrequently, actions attributed to Jahwe appeared derogatory in later ages; and hence, therefore, the "toning down" process which is often observable in the Old Testament. Jahwe thus appears in these passages as divine-human,

SUMMARY OF THE MATERIAL DEALT WITH

in the character of " Heilbringer." Analogous figures among other peoples of a " Saviour-Hero " prove the wide prevalence of the idea, and the probability therefore of the Hebrew writers utilizing material which in its essence was the common property of the world.

In the *Paradise-myth*, or " Golden Age " myth, there were seen to be two complementary parts, though in the first instance its form must have been simpler; it is concerned with the distant past and with the future. The underlying idea is that long ago gods and men lived happily together, there was sufficiency of food, there was ease and comfort, and universal peace reigned—the very animals were all at peace with one another. A divine personality, who had, however, some human characteristics, ruled over men in justice and equity. There was a specified locality which was the scene of this happy era, the return of which at some future time was looked for.

These are the main points, though some others of less importance occur as well, and will be referred to as occasion requires.

II.

THE THOUGHT-SEQUENCE OF THE THREE MYTHS.

A matter of some importance for the present argument must here be briefly alluded to; the fact, namely, that the main substance of these three myths forms a logical sequence. This is a point of considerable interest, for it goes to support the contention that the three myths in question are the expression of innate feelings in man. It will have been noticed that in the various forms of the *Tehom*-myth it is almost invariably implied in the myth itself that it refers to the first beginnings of things ; this, as has been shown, applies also to the Old Testament account. It may therefore be asserted that the *Tehom*-myth was the earliest of the three which was formulated. This agrees with what one would expect from all that is known of the " Gemüth " of early man ; the emotion of superstitious fear is, apart from the purely animal cravings of the desire to live and to propagate the species, that which was dominant in him when he had reached that stage in his mental evolution in which this sensation was capable of becoming articulate. The myth, therefore, of a cruel monster, intimately bound up with the element of water, was the first of the three which came to be formulated. But it stands in the very nature of things that man cannot for very long acquiesce in the belief of an evil or harmful power alone ; however dire and calamitous his environment, there is on the one hand the fact, which must have occurred to some natures, that no matter how bad things are, they are never so bad but that they might

SUMMARY OF THE MATERIAL DEALT WITH

be worse—and, on the other hand, the innate, though it may be at first inarticulate, conviction that there must be some power to balance the evil one. The fact of a belief in the existence of an evil power demands a corresponding belief in the existence of a beneficent one ; even if this were not self-evident, the proof of its truth could be seen in every religious system that the world has ever heard of, the most primitive as well as the most spiritual.[1] And therefore one may unhesitatingly assert that some early form of the " Jahwe-myth " came second in order among the three under consideration. But, once more, the mind of early man would have demanded some, to him, satisfying proof that the Beneficent Power really was what he yearned for, one namely who was more powerful than the cruel monster, the belief in whose existence had so long darkened his heart ; if this Beneficent Power was not *more* powerful than the evil one, he could be of no use to man. Therefore it became part of the myth that at the beginning of things a great

[1] This is not meant to imply that there necessarily existed in such systems something which corresponded to the later Dualism of Zoroastrian belief ; on the contrary, as will be seen below, early Israelite belief, for example, from the first, never regarded the two opposing powers as balanced against one another ; the evil power is always subordinate, and it is taken for granted that its final disappearance is only a matter of time.

THE EVOLUTION OF THE MESSIANIC IDEA

conflict took place between these two powers, and that the Beneficent Power conquered the evil one; though he could not have finally destroyed it, because it was still often in evidence. A further development took place when the conviction arose that ultimately the Beneficent Power must triumph, and the cruel monster be destroyed for ever. But there was another element in this myth; it was, again, in the nature of things that early man should inquire as to the why and wherefore, the whence and how, of all the good and useful things that he saw around him; and the obvious reply to his inquiries would have been that the Beneficent Power who overcame the primeval cruel monster was the author of these blessings. Thus the "Dragon-slayer" became also the "Heilbringer." A characteristic of the "Heilbringer" was that he was in some sense a Creator, for to him men would ascribe the origin of themselves, as well as that of other things, when once they began to think about such things; the result was that this Beneficent Power was conceived of as a personality both divine and human.

One more step; one of the first results of the victory of the Beneficent Power over the primeval cruel power was, according to the simple mind of primitive man, the putting in order of the world in general, and then of the forming of men by

SUMMARY OF THE MATERIAL DEALT WITH

the divine-human " Heilbringer." But the obvious question would have suggested itself as to where the " Heilbringer " lived and what he did with the men he had formed. The answer could not have been long in coming ; the " Heilbringer " lived in his own domain of luxuriant beauty, and the men he had formed, of course, lived with him ; and since the evil power had been overcome, and the Beneficent Power who lived among men was supreme, all the world was happy, and all men lived at ease, and he who ruled over them was good, and gave them all they wanted. The problem which presented itself to later ages as to why this happy time should ever have come to an end was answered in many different ways ; but however much they may have lamented its disappearance, there was always the thought of comfort, that some time or other in the future it would come again, when the Beneficent Power would again show his strength, this time by finally destroying the evil monster.

The picture thus presented of the supposed sequence of thought among early men which, in accordance with some of their elemental characteristics, resulted in these myths, may or may not approximate to what actually happened ; but it will probably be conceded that in the myths as we now have them a sequence of some kind may be discerned. As from age to age new elements

THE EVOLUTION OF THE MESSIANIC IDEA

found expression in the myths, and their form became more and more modified, two results followed; in the first place, the thought-sequence tended to become obscured, and in the second place, a certain inter-mixture between the myths themselves took place. In the later stage of their history, therefore, as presented to us in the Old Testament, it is inevitable that they should appear to a large extent interwoven and interdependent; this is what one would, in any case, have expected; for which reason such a passage, for example, as Isaiah li. 9-11 is, in this connexion, exceedingly instructive, for here the echoes of all three myths resound, and moreover, in the order in which the thought-sequence, as outlined above, would demand. Thus in verse 9*b* the words, *Art not thou that which clave in pieces Rahab, that pierced the Dragon?* recall how *Tehom* was overcome; in verse 11*a* the words, *The ransomed of Jahwe shall return, and come with singing unto Zion*, are a faint re-echo, adapted to later events, of Jahwe in the character of " Heilbringer " ; and in verse 11*bc* the words, *And everlasting joy shall be upon their heads: they shall obtain gladness and joy, and sorrow and sighing shall flee away*, contain a distinct picture of the main characteristic of the " Paradise " or "Golden Age" myth. Instances of this kind can be found elsewhere, e.g. Isaiah xxxv. 3-10; they emphasize the fact that in the

SUMMARY OF THE MATERIAL DEALT WITH

Old Testament these three myths have become interwoven and interdependent.

Another point of importance which must be emphasized is that in the history of such myths as those under consideration, which reaches far back into pre-historical times, many links in the development of ideas have become lost in transmission. It could not be otherwise, for the mental evolution of man in a low stage of civilization is of necessity very slow ; the steps are imperceptible ; to speak metaphorically, the links are in process of dissolution as soon as they are forged. There seems to be but one way—and that but too often inadequate —open to us to-day whereby it becomes possible to fill up gaps in the history of ideas, and to surmise what was probably the nature of the lost links which joined together the different stages in the evolution of thought ; and that is by observing the several stages of an analogous idea among peoples in various grades of culture. It is for this reason that the three myths dealt with were considered in a variety of forms above. But further ; when traditional beliefs came to be written down, the process, already referred to, of eliminating what to later ages appeared incongruous or unfitting became a far more drastic means of dissolving the links than the more or less unconscious one referred to above ; so that when dealing with the history and development

THE EVOLUTION OF THE MESSIANIC IDEA

of ideas in the Old Testament we are faced with grave difficulties, which can never be wholly overcome; for this reason, in seeking for lost links in the historical chain of an idea, conjecture, based whenever possible upon analogy, becomes not only permissible, but even necessary. In the following chapters, therefore, these considerations must be allowed due weight.

CHAPTER XIII.

SATAN.

The meaning of this word in the Old Testament; the difference in meaning in the older and later literature; suggested theory as to the reason of this difference—Further considerations: correspondence between the characteristics of *Tehom* and Satan; the prophetical teaching concerning the personality of God, and consequent development of the sense of sin; growing perception of the meaning of opposition to God—*Tehom*, the embodiment of harmfulness developed into Satan, the embodiment of the principle of evil—Adaptation of earlier material, with some examples from pseudepigraphic literature, etc.—Theories as to the original of evil and its existence in the world; the "Yetser hara'"—The end of *Tehom* (Satan) predicted—The final development of the "Tehom-myth" in the *Apocalypse*.

The Hebrew root (*shaṭan*) from which this word comes means "to oppose," or "to act as an adversary"; this sense is brought out clearly in Num. xxii. 22, where the noun is used: *And the Angel of Jahwe* (the Septuagint reads, "The angel of God") *placed himself in the way* (the Septuagint omits "in the way") *for an adversary to him* (lit., "as a Satan to him"); the Septuagint ἐνδιαβαγεῖν, "to bedevil," is instructive (see further Num. xxii. 32). In the few other passages in the earlier literature (1 Sam. xxix. 4; 2 Sam. xix. 23 [22, E.V.]; 1 Kings v. 18 [4 E.V.], xi. 14,

23, 25) in which the word occurs it has always the sense of "adversary" (Septuagint, "devil," ὁ διάβολος). In Psalm cix. 6, which is late, the word has assumed a considerably developed meaning, that namely of "accuser," but in an evil sense, for it is paralleled with the "wicked man" in the first half of the verse. In all the other passages in which the word occurs (1 Chron. xxi. 1; Job i. 2; Zech. iii. 1, 2) it has become a proper name, and refers to a distinct personality. The characteristics of this personality in these passages are as follows :—He moves men to sin; he is super-human, though his activity is represented as being exercised among men on earth, where he has power to do men bodily as well as spiritual harm; he is subject to God, to Whom, however, he stands in opposition. One of the first things that strikes one here is the immense gap there is between the simple meaning of "opposer," which attaches to the word in the earlier literature, and the development which has taken place in the later books; there is no bridge over the chasm which divides these two stages. This fact is possibly to be accounted for in the following way: up to the Exile the word "Satan" —not in itself a very common word—was used in the general sense of "adversary" or "opposer"; during the Exile the Israelites' ancient belief concerning those myths (among others), which

TEHOM AND SATAN

have been referred to above, received renewed vigour from the more luxuriant forms of them among the Babylonians ; but, at the same time, the more spiritual tendency which had been fostered ever since the rise of the greater prophets (Amos, Hosea, Isaiah, etc.) induced the Israelite teachers to present these myths to their people in a more spiritualized form. *Tehom*, who had opposed Jahwe in the beginning, who had been His adversary, as well as man's, in the garden of Eden, and who had been the enemy of God and men at the time of the Flood when again he had appeared in the character of Opposer,—*Tehom* became the "Opposer" or "Satan" *par excellence*. Thus, although before the Exile the word "Satan" might be used of any adversary indiscriminately, after the Exile it would have been specifically applied to one who, according to ancient belief, had been from the very beginning the enemy of God and men ; from this to the use of the word as a proper name was not only an easy, but an inevitable transition. Some further considerations must be brought forward in this connexion.

The general correspondence between the main characteristics of *Tehom* and *Satan* go far to prove that the underlying ideas expressed by either term are related in the closest possible way. The enmity of *Tehom* towards Jahwe has been

THE EVOLUTION OF THE MESSIANIC IDEA

dealt with in an earlier chapter, and need therefore only be referred to in passing. In early Israel this fact would not have denoted sinfulness on the part of *Tehom*, because the conception of sin, as it was conceived of in later times, had not yet arisen ; but *Tehom* was the embodiment of *harmfulness ;* impotent of course towards God, but well able to injure men (cf. above, Am. ix. 3, Gen. iii. 15-19, vii. 11, 12, 21-24 and Chapter IV). With the teaching of the prophets, however, came an entirely new conception of the Personality of God, and with it a correspondingly advanced conception with regard to enmity towards Him ; that is to say, a growing sense of Sin ; " when we turn to the prophetical teaching on Sin we find, indeed, that an immense advance has taken place ; the whole relationship between God and man has undergone a great change ; the ethical standpoint of the prophets is immeasurably higher than what went before ; the conception of God and His holiness is utterly different from the beliefs of earlier times ; moral, and ritual offences are not merely differentiated, but they are seen in their true proportion." [1] These two concurrent ideas of the majesty and holiness of God, and the sinfulness of man, must have induced a great change

[1] Oesterley and Box, *The Religion and Worship of the Synagogue*, p. 232 (1907) ; cf. the whole of chap. xii. § 1, " The Teaching of the Old Testament " (i.e., on Sin).

SATAN

to come about regarding anything in the shape of opposition to God. Hence the idea hitherto held with regard to *Tehom* as to his being the embodiment of evil, in the sense of *harm-doing*, developed into that of his being the embodiment of evil in the sense of *wickedness*. When, therefore, "Satan" came to be used as a kind of *terminus technicus* for the primeval cruel monster, the name connoted that which was sinful; and when, further, the development took place according to which a distinctive personality became attached to the name, then that personality, of course, became the embodiment of the principle of evil, in the sense of Sin.

With these advancing ideas among Israel's teachers one can well understand that there arose a gradual realization of the fact that the ancient beliefs were not in all respects consonant with the higher spiritual conceptions which had arisen; the tendency, therefore, to modify the form, at all events, of these traditional beliefs must have been constantly on the increase; this would explain, for example, how the name *Tehom* was gradually dropped, and that of *Satan* took its place. But, on the other hand, however great the desire to eradicate what was considered false, popular attachment to ancient traditions would have been far too strong to permit of *complete* success to the enlightened spirits of the

THE EVOLUTION OF THE MESSIANIC IDEA

age ; so that it would have been found absolutely necessary to utilize the ancient material. In this way the process of adaptation went on for centuries, so that even in post-biblical (Pseudepigraphic) literature, as well as in early Christian writings, the ancient myths are still in evidence as far as their outward form was concerned.

This principle of adapting old ideas to new beliefs has been already referred to. A few references may be given to illustrate what has been said. In the *Book of Jubilees* it is told how that after the Flood, demons, who (according to x. 11) are under the leadership of Satan,[1] came and tempted the grandchildren of Noah to sin ; Noah prayed to God, Who thereupon commanded that all the demons, with the exception of one tenth, were to be consigned to the " Place of Condemnation " ; the remaining tenth part were permitted to tempt the children of men to evil under the leadership of Satan (*Book of Jubilees* x. 1-11). With this should be compared what was said in Chapter VII. ii. The idea of Satan having a number of subordinate helpers is paralleled by a similar thing in Zoroastrian

[1] In x. 8, *Mastēma* is spoken of as the prince of demons, but the meaning of this word, according to Dillmann, is derived from a word meaning " Accuser " ; this is a characteristic of Satan ; but see Charles's note (in his edition), which quotes the original Hebrew expression from the Book of Noah (Midrashic). The passage x. 8–11, taken as a whole, shows that only one person is denoted under these two names.

SATAN IN PSEUDEPIGRAPHA

belief, where Angra-Mainyu is represented as being assisted by a number of fiends; we find the same thing in Babylonian belief in the " brood of Tiamat" (cf. Ps. lxxiv. 13, lxxxix. 10-11). Satan with this following, bent on causing men to sin, is further referred to in the *Martyrdom of Isaiah* ii. 1 ff.[1] In the *Book of Enoch* there is a significant passage, which, although it is a fragment from the *Book of Noah*, is important owing to the context in which it has been placed; in speaking of the " hosts of Azazel," [2] who are to be cast into the " Abyss of Condemnation," it says: " That the Lord of Spirits may take vengeance on them for their unrighteousness in becoming subject to Satan and leading astray those who dwell on the earth "; then follows the Noachic fragment: " And in those days will punishment come from the Lord of Spirits, and all the chambers of waters which are above the heavens will be opened and of the fountains which are below the heavens and beneath the earth. And all the waters will be joined with the waters: that which is above the heavens is the masculine and the water which is beneath the earth is the feminine. And all who dwell on the earth will be

[1] Sammael, who is mentioned here, is identical with Satan, see the passage in question; cf. the present writer's article on "Demonology" in Hastings' *Dict. of Christ and the Gospels*, i. 439b.

[2] Also to be identified with Satan.

destroyed and those who dwell under the ends of heaven. And they will thereby recognize their unrighteousness which they have committed on the earth, and owing to this they will be destroyed."[1] The chief point of interest in this passage is that sinful men are those who are subject to Satan, whereupon immediately there follows the account of the waters of *Tehom-Rabbah* breaking forth and slaying men in punishment for sin; the connexion between Satan as the embodiment of sin and *Tehom-Rabbah* as the means used for punishing sin, seems therefore close. The passage also seems to indicate that the identification between Satan and *Tehom* had long been recognized. But the passages in which the process of adaptation comes out most clearly, and from which it can be distinctly seen that the ancient *Tehom*, the cruel primeval monster, has been supplanted by Satan, are to be found in the *Apocalypse*, viz.: *And the great dragon was cast down, the old serpent, he that is called the Devil and Satan, the deceiver of the whole world; he was cast down to the earth, and his angels were cast down with him* (xii. 9); in the original Hebrew form[2] we have here some words which the investigation of this subject has made familiar, viz.: " The

[1] liv. 4–10. (Ed. Charles.)
[2] This is not intended to imply that the *whole* of the Apocalypse was originally written in Hebrew, but only certain parts of it; cf. Swete's edition.

THE APOCALYPSE

Great Dragon," " The old Serpent," " Satan " ; in the next verse he is spoken of as " the Accuser of our brethren." Still more striking, as showing the way in which the ancient *Tehom*-myth has been adapted, are verses 13 ff. of the same chapter : *And when the dragon saw that he was cast down to the earth he persecuted the woman which brought forth the man child. . . . And the serpent cast out of his mouth after the woman water as a river, that he might cause her to be carried away by the stream.* . . . Here the Dragon, identified with the Serpent, is brought into direct connexion with the destructive watery element (i.e. *Tehom-Rabbah*) ; and, once more, in xx. 1-2 we read : *And I saw an angel coming down out of heaven, having the key of the abyss and a great chain in his hand. And he laid hold of the dragon, the old serpent, which is the Devil and Satan, and bound him for a thousand years.* . . . These few examples will be sufficient to show that Satan, the personification of evil, is the development of *Tehom*, the primeval cruel monster ; and that the *Tehom*-myth has been adapted in order to instruct later generations in the doctrine of Sin.

But two other points require yet to be touched upon. It was seen to be a constant note in the echoes of the *Tehom*-myth, in almost all its various forms, that *Tehom* was conquered, but not finally destroyed ; the reason of this element in the myth was probably, as already pointed out, due to the fact that there were but too many traces still existing of his power. At a certain (late) stage in the history of the myth, however, it became apparently a difficult problem to reconcile this with the power and majesty of God which more spiritual beliefs had brought about ; as a result (or at all events this problem must have had something to do with it) certain theories were propounded as to the origin and existence of sin in the world, which, while recognizing the presence of Satan (the counter-part of *Tehom*), sought to fasten upon *men* the real cause of the continued existence of sin. A clear trace of such a theory is to be found, for example, in the book of *The life of Adam and Eve* ; in § 19 of that work we read as follows : " When she (i.e. the Serpent) had received my oath, she came and ascended into it (i.e. the tree). But she placed within the fruit which she gave me to eat, the poison of her wickedness, that is, her lust ; for lust is the beginning of all sin. And she bent the bough to the earth, and I took of the fruit and ate."[1] We have here an interesting example of the Jewish doctrine of the *Yetzer hara'* ; the theory which this doctrine gives expression to was " probably prevalent long before its appearance in Rabbinical literature, and seems to be taught in the Book

[1] Ed. Kautzsch.

THE YETZER HARA'

of *Sirach* (*Ecclesiasticus*), e.g. xvi. 11, xxi. 31, xxxvii. 3. The extraordinary thing about this theory of the origin of sin is that, in the last instance, God is the cause of Sin; for, as Creator of all things, He created the *Yetzer hara'* in Adam, the existence of which made the Fall possible (*Bereshith Rabbah*, c. 27). A few passages may be cited to show this. The Almighty is made to say: 'I grieve that I created man of earthly substance; for had I created him of heavenly substance, he would not have rebelled against Me' (*Yalkut Shim. Beresh.* xliv. 47); again: 'It repenteth Me that I created the *Yetzer hara'* in man, for had I not done this he would not have rebelled against Me' (*ibid.* 61); once more: 'I created an *evil tendency*. I created for him (i.e. man) the Law as a means of healing. If ye occupy yourselves with (the study of) the Law, ye will not fall into the power of it (i.e. the *evil tendency*)'" (*Kiddushin* 30b).[1] In the meantime the *Tehom*-myth was still current. But the belief in God's Omnipotence brought with it the conviction that, sooner or later, the principle of evil, as centred now in Satan, would be entirely annihilated. A few references to this may be indicated: " And all their days shall they accomplish and live in peace and happiness, *for Satan shall be no more, nor evil, to harm them*" (*Book of*

[1] Oesterley and Box, *op. cit.* p. 242.

Jubilees, xxiii. 29) ; " And then shall appear His Kingdom in all His creation, and then Zabulus shall have an end, and sorrow shall depart with him" (*Assumption of Moses* x. 1) ; in the same chapter, verse 6, occur these significant words : " And the Sea shall ebb even to the abyss and the fountains of waters shall fail, and his floods shall dry up " ;[1] *cf.* the words, " the waters being dried up " (*Test. Levi* iv.). This destruction of the *Sea* is spoken of again in the *Sybilline Oracles* v. 158, 159 : " But there shall descend from Heaven into the terrible Salt-sea a great star and he shall burn up the great deep " ; and in verse 447 we read : " And in the last times the Sea shall dry up," cf. 530 ; the " burning up " of the Sea is also referred to in iii. 84–85 of the same work.[2] It is only a different way of expressing the same idea when the principle of evil is spoken of as coming to an end, as, for example, in *Enoch* x. 22 : " And the earth will be cleansed from all corruption, and from all sin. . . ." ; 4 *Esdr.* vi. 27–28 : " Then shall evil be destroyed, and deceit annihilated ; but faith shall flourish,

[1] Ed. Charles.
[2] Cf. the vision of the Man from the Sea (4 Esdr. xiii. 2-13), where the Man, having conquered the " Sea " (= Tehom), comes and destroys the wicked ; a great deal might be said here regarding this passage, which is very *à propos* ; it should be read in full. See the writer's article in *The International Journal of Apocrypha*, Jan., 1908.

corruption vanquished, and truth which for so long has been without fruit, shall be displayed "; cf. *Pss. of Sol.* xvii. 21 ff.; *Rom.* xvi. 20; 2 *Thess.* ii. 8. But the most striking passage in which this final overthrow of evil is referred to, and where it is also described in the imagery of the ancient myth, is the following : *And there was war in Heaven : Michael and his angels going forth to war with the dragon ; and the dragon warred and his angels ; and they prevailed not, neither was their place found any more in Heaven. And the great dragon was cast down, the old serpent, he that is called the Devil and Satan, the deceiver of the whole world ; he was cast down to the earth, and his angels were cast down with him. And I heard a great voice in Heaven, saying, Now is come the salvation, and the power, and the Kingdom of our God, and the authority of his Christ ; for the accuser of our brethren is cast down, which accuseth them before our God day and night* (*Apoc.* xii. 7–10) ; but the central point, for our present purpose, lies in the words that follow : *And they overcame him because of the blood of the Lamb* ; the victory is brought about by the *Messiah*. It is for this reason that the *Tehom*-myth finds its place in a discussion on the " Messianic Idea." But even now the final scene has not taken place, for it goes on in verse 12 : *Woe for the earth and for the sea : because the devil is gone down unto you, having great wrath, knowing that he hath but a short time*; this short time is referred to again in xx. 1–3 : *And I saw an angel coming down out of heaven, having the key of the abyss and a great chain in his hand. And he laid hold on the dragon, the old serpent, which is the Devil and Satan, and bound him for a thousand years, and cast him into the abyss, and shut it, and sealed it over him, that he should deceive the nations no more, until the thousand years should be finished ; after this he must be loosed for a little time*; see further xx. 7–8 ; then in verse 10 comes the conclusion : *And the devil that deceived them was cast into the lake of fire and brimstone, where are also the beast and the false prophet ; and they shall be tormented day and night for ever and ever.* The final destruction of evil is again referred to in xxi. 1, in the language of the *Tehom*-myth : *And I saw a new heaven and a new earth : for the first heaven and the first earth are passed away ;* AND THE SEA IS NO MORE. That the victory is achieved by the Messiah is seen by the mention of the *Lamb* in the remainder of the chapter.

There are, of course, other elements in the chapters of the *Apocalypse* from which these passages are taken, as there are indeed also in some of the passages themselves ; but with these we are not concerned here.

Thus the *Tehom*-myth, modified and adapted

SATAN

more and more as the ages passed on, had from the beginning contained the germ of a truth which is eternal. In whatever different guises that truth may have appeared in order that it might be capable of reception by different generations of men among whom there was a constant growth in spiritual conception, its root-idea remained the same—evil, which was destined finally to be overcome by good. It could therefore, in allegorical form, be utilized in the Christian Church to teach the eternal truth of the victory of Christ, the Messiah, over the powers of evil.

CHAPTER XIV.

THE MESSIAH.

THE use and meaning of the word " Messiah " in the Old Testament—The examination of some Biblical passages in which the ancient " Heilbringer " conception appears to have been adapted and applied to the Messiah—Signs of development—Isa. ii. 2–4*a* ; Isa. iv. 2–6—The " Branch of Jahwe "—The doctrine of the " Remnant "—Isa. ix. 5, 6.

[LITERATURE :—As indicated in the footnotes.]

BEFORE coming to consider some of the Messianic passages in the Old Testament in which pre-existing myth-material has been utilized and adapted to higher teaching, a brief note on the word " Messiah " will not be out of place.

The root from which the word comes (*mashah*) is used, in its verbal form, in the following ways : firstly, in the sense of " to smear," both of things and persons ; thus in Jeremiah xxii. 14 it is used of painting a house with vermilion (משוח בששר) ; in Isaiah xxi. 5 (assuming that the text is correct) it is used of " anointing the shield " ; this custom, though in later times practised for purposes of practical utility, denoted probably in its origin something more significant ; weapons of war were consecrated on the same principle upon which warriors consecrated themselves for war ; the expression, " to sanctify war " (Mic. iii. 5 ; Jer. vi. 4,

THE MEANING OF THE WORD *MESSIAH*

etc.), bears this out. Other inanimate things in connexion with which the word is used are: the standing stone: (*I am the God of Bethel, where thou anointedst a pillar* . . ., Gen. xxxi. 13); the altar: (. . . *And thou shalt anoint it*, i.e. the altar, *to sanctify it*, Exod. xxix. 36); the tabernacle, the ark, and various holy vessels, Exodus xxx. 26–29; Leviticus viii. 10, 11; and also unleavened cakes: (. . . *and wafers unleavened anointed with oil*, Exod. xxix. 2; Lev. ii. 4; Num. vi. 15); in a much later time also it is used of anointing the Most Holy Place (*to anoint the Holy of Holies*, Dan. ix. 24). In all these instances the idea of consecrating to holy uses is prominent. But it is in its use in connexion with *persons* that the importance of the word is more especially seen. As in the case of *things* there is only one instance of its use in a non-technical sense (i.e. Jer. xxii. 14), so too when it is used of *persons* there is but one instance of this, namely in Amos vi. 6, where the reference is to the self-indulgence and luxury of the rich, who " anoint themselves with the chief ointments." Its normal use is in connexion with anointing for the purpose of consecration, and here it is to be noted that the consecration is to the offices of *prophet, king*, and *priest*. A few examples may be offered: in reference to anointing to the prophetical office we have the case of Elijah anointing Elisha, (. . . *and Elisha the son of Shaphat of*

THE EVOLUTION OF THE MESSIANIC IDEA

Abel-meholah shalt thou anoint to be prophet in thy stead, 1 Kings xix. 16), and in Isaiah lxi. 1 the reference is also clearly to the prophetical office (*The spirit of the Lord God is upon me ; because the Lord hath anointed me to preach good tidings to the poor. . . .*). The use of the word, however, in connexion with the prophetical office is rare ; with that of the kingship, on the other hand, it frequently occurs, e.g. in the parable in Judges ix. 8 : "The trees went forth on a time to anoint a king over them" ; 1 Kings i. 45 : *And Zadok the priest and Nathan the prophet having anointed him King in Gihon* ; Psalm lxxxix. 21 (20 in Heb.) : *I have found David my servant ; with my holy oil have I anointed him* ; see further 1 Samuel xvi. 3 ; 2 Kings xi. 12, xxiii. 30, etc., etc. Less frequent, and belonging mostly to literature of a later date, are the passages which speak of the anointing to the priesthood ; e.g. in Exodus xxviii. 41 the command is given that men are to be anointed to the priest's office : . . . *And thou shalt anoint them and consecrate them* (lit., " fill their hand "), *and sanctify them that they may minister unto me in the priest's office* ; so too Exodus xxix. 7, where the mode of consecration is seen to be identical with that of consecration to the kingship : *Then shalt thou take the anointing oil, and pour it upon his head, and anoint him* ; see, further, Exodus xl. 13, 15 ; Leviticus vii. 36, viii. 12 ; Numbers iii. 3.

THE MEANING OF THE WORD *MESSIAH*

The noun " Messiah " (*Māshiaḥ*) is used in reference to the *King* who is called " the Anointed," or " Messiah " of Jahwe (1 Sam. ii. 10. xxiv. 7, 11 ; Hab. iii. 13, etc.) ; in reference to the *High-priest*, lit. " the priest, the Messiah," Leviticus iv. 3, 5, 16, etc. ; of *Cyrus* (*Thus saith Jahwe to his anointed, to Cyrus.* . . .), Isaiah xlv. 1 ; of the *Messianic prince* (*Know therefore and discern, that from the going forth of the commandment to restore and to build Jerusalem, unto the anointed one, the prince, shall be seven weeks.* . . .), Daniel ix. 25, 26 ; of the *Patriarchs* (*Touch not mine anointed ones, and do my prophets no harm*), Psalm cv. 15, which must be read with the context ; and of *Zerubbabel*, see Haggai ii. 23 ; Zechariah iii. 8, vi. 12.

The question as to the original idea underlying the act of anointing is one which naturally suggests itself here, and in replying to it no better course could be taken than that of quoting the very instructive words of Robertson Smith on the subject : " The Hebrew word meaning 'to anoint ' (*mashaḥ*) means properly to wipe or stroke with the hand, which was used to spread the unguent over the skin. Thus the anointing of the sacred symbol is associated with the simpler form of homage common in Arabia, in which the hand was passed over the idol. . . . The ultimate source of the use of unguents in religion " is

THE EVOLUTION OF THE MESSIANIC IDEA

discussed in a later passage, where he says, further :
" In the later fire-rituals, the fat of the victim, with its blood, is quite specially the altar food of the gods. But between the practice which this view represents and the primitive practice, in which the whole body was eaten, we must, I think, in accordance with what has just been said, insert an intermediate stage, which can still be seen and studied in the usage of primitive peoples. Among the Damaras the fat of particular animals ' is supposed to possess certain virtues, and is carefully collected and kept in vessels of a particular kind. A small portion dissolved in water is given to persons who return home safely after a lengthened absence ; . . . the chief makes use of it as an unguent for his body.' [1] So too 'dried flesh and fat' are used as amulets by the Namaquas.[2] Among the Bechuanas lubrication with grease is part of the ceremony of admission of girls into womanhood, and among the Hottentots young men on their initiation into manhood are daubed with fat and soot.[3] Grease is the usual unguent all over Africa, and from these examples we see that its use is not merely hygienic, but has a sacred meaning. Indeed, the use of various kinds of fat, especially human fat, as a charm, is common all over the world, and we learn from the

[1] Anderson, *Lake Ngami*, p. 223.
[2] Ibid. p. 330.   [3] Ibid. p. 465.

THE MEANING OF THE WORD *MESSIAH*

Australian superstition, quoted above,[1] that the reason of this is that the fat, as a special seat of life, is a vehicle of the living virtue of the being from which it is taken. Now we have seen, in speaking of the use of unguents in Semitic religion, that this particular medium has in some way an equivalent value to blood, for which it may be substituted in the covenant ceremony, and also in the ceremony of bedaubing the sacred stone as an act of homage. If, now, we remember that the oldest unguents are animal fats, and that vegetable oil was unknown to the Semitic nomads,[2] we are plainly led to the conclusion that unction is primarily an application of the sacrificial fat, with its living virtues, to the persons of the worshippers. On this view the anointing of kings, and the use of unguents on visiting the sanctuary, are at once intelligible."[3] The anointed king was therefore one who, by means of the anointing, received living virtues. But these

---

[1] Viz. : " When the Australians kill an enemy in blood revenge, ' they always abstract the kidney fat, and also take off a piece of the skin of the thigh ' (or a piece of the flank). ' These are carried home as trophies. . . . The caul fat is carefully kept by the assassin, and used to lubricate himself ' ; he thinks, we are told, that thus the strength of the victim enters into him."

[2] Fränkel, *Fremdwörter*, p. 147.

[3] *The Religion of the Semites* (new edition, 1894), pp. 233, 382–384.

living virtues, which the sacrificial fat was supposed to contain, cannot have been conceived of as existing simply because the fat had been offered up in sacrifice. We have here, rather, something analogous to the idea that because a kinship existed between certain clans, animals and gods, that therefore in partaking of the flesh of particular animals sacrificed on especial occasions, the worshippers were united to their god [1]; that is to say, that as the virtue of the god is transferred to the worshipper by his eating what is practically the flesh of the god, so, in the same way, the "living virtues" which accrued to one who was anointed with the sacrificial fat, were due to the fact that he had been anointed with what was part of the deity. This exceedingly antique idea must have been the remote ancestor of the highly spiritualized belief of " unction " being the symbol of the spirit of God coming upon a man. And if this is so the passage in Isaiah xi. 1 ff. has peculiar interest: *And there shall come forth a shoot out of the stock of Jesse . . . and the spirit of Jahwe shall rest upon him, etc.* (see below).

In turning now to examine a few passages in which the ancient conception of a " Heilbringer " has been adapted and applied to the Messiah, a

[1] Cf. the various chapters on Sacrifice in the work quoted, and Frazer's *The Golden Bough* (2nd Ed.), § 11, " Eating the god," and § 12, " Killing the Divine Animal," ii. pp. 318–448.

ISAIAH II. 2-4A

very great development in spiritual thought will naturally be looked for, and found. Not only so, but the material used will necessarily be coloured by a variety of ideas which belonged to the Hebrews, or, more specifically, to their religious leaders; so that in the few examples to be given some new elements appear, and these must be briefly dealt with in passing, in order that the passages in question may be adequately examined; the slight digressions occasioned in consequence will not be out of place if they in any way contribute to the elucidation of the verses discussed.

Isaiah ii. 2–4a : *And it shall come to pass in the latter end of the days that the mount of Jahwe* (so the Septuagint, omitting בית, τὸ ὄρος κυρίου) *shall be firmly grounded on the top of the mountains, and shall be lifted up* (*higher than*) *the hills, and all the nations shall flow unto it; yea, many nations shall go, saying : " Come, and let us ascend up unto the mount of Jahwe, even unto the house of the God of Jacob, that he may teach us of his ways, and that we may walk in his paths; for out of Zion shall come forth instruction, and the word of Jahwe out of Jerusalem. And he shall judge among the nations, and shall decide concerning many peoples.*[1]

[1] Verse 4b, which belongs to this passage, will be discussed in Chapter XVI., to which it more appropriately belongs.

THE EVOLUTION OF THE MESSIANIC IDEA

The subject of the mount of Jahwe has already been referred to above; we shall have to return to it in Chapter XVI. Originally this mount had, as we have seen, nothing to do with mount Zion or Jerusalem, but the ancient conception of the abode of the gods upon a mount in the North, where Paradise was supposed to be located, is adapted by the prophet, and is described as in the very heart of the land of Israel. But the point that concerns us here is that *Jahwe* is spoken of as the ruler and the judge. We have seen reason to believe that the early idea of " Heilbringer " was attributed to Jahwe, and that it was He Who brought material blessings to His people. In the passage before us this is developed and spiritualized, and Jahwe is represented as concerned with the *spiritual* welfare of men. In most of the forms of the antecedent myth the " Heilbringer " associates more or less with His people; this *trait* still finds a place in the passage before us; Jahwe is represented as dwelling on earth in the time to come; but instead of teaching them arts or the like, He will instruct them in righteousness and in living at peace with each other. The " Universalism " which characterizes this passage is likewise a development; the " Heilbringer " of ancient conception was one who was concerned with his own people; here the whole world is embraced. A " particularistic " note is, however,

ISAIAH II. 2-4A

sounded in that the land of Israel is to be the scene of Jahwe's beneficent activity. It is a point to be particularly noted that the ruler during the peaceful and happy time to come is *Jahwe* ; this is strictly in accord with what was to be expected from what has been said above in Chapters VIII, IX, for in almost every form of the antecedent myth the " Heilbringer " who helps his people, dwells among them, and is of a Divine-human nature. In the passage we are considering the words are no doubt meant to be taken in a metaphorical sense, but the idea that lies behind them is that of Jahwe dwelling on His mount and receiving all who come to Him, in order to teach them personally. It is here that the adaptation of pre-existing myth-material comes out so clearly. The people had been for centuries intimately acquainted with this floating material, and this prophet, so vastly superior to them in spiritual discernment, seeks to inculcate a higher teaching. It was not only natural and fitting, but it was the only course open to him to use as the point of attachment that with which his hearers were familiar ; his representation of Jahwe is not the most exalted (here, at any rate), as must be clear when comparing this passage with some others which deal with His personality (e.g. vi. 1-13), but it is greatly in advance of what the conceptions of his people must have been, from all that we know of these; and therefore he represents Jahwe in a character not wholly unfamiliar, but as much more spiritual and exalted than the popular conceptions regarding Him.

Isaiah iv. 2–6 : (2) *In that day the Branch of Jahwe shall be beautiful and glorious, and the fruit of the land shall be excellent and comely for them that are escaped of Israel.* (3) *And it shall come to pass, that he that is left in Zion, and he that remaineth in Jerusalem, shall be called holy, every one that is written among the living in Jerusalem;* (4) *when Jahwe shall have washed away the filth of the daughters of Zion, and shall have purged the blood of Jerusalem from the midst of her with the spirit of judgment and with the spirit of burning.* (5) *And Jahwe shall come* (so the Septuagint, followed by the old Latin Version and the Syro-Hexapla) *upon all the dwelling-place of Mount Zion and upon all its surrounding land* (cf. the Septuagint and the Syro-Hexapla) *(in) a cloud by day and smoke, and (in) the shining of a flaming fire by night; and over the glory of Jahwe a canopy;* (6) *and a pavilion there shall be for shade from the heat* [in the day-time] (the Septuagint and the Syro-Hexapla omit "in the day-time"), *and for a refuge and for a covert from storm and from rain.*

The text at the end of verse 5 and beginning of 6 is evidently in a corrupt state, and it is not easy to get an altogether satisfactory translation;

ISAIAH IV. 2-6

the meaning, however, is fairly clear, and before dealing with the rest of the verse, it may be well to consider briefly the conception presented here, that, namely, of the *Shekhinah*. This word comes from the root *shakan*, "to dwell" or "to abide"; although the actual word does not occur in the Old Testament, its underlying idea may be discerned in a number of places. "The origin of the *Shekhinah*, in its technical sense, is to be found in such Old Testament passages as Exodus xl. 34 ff., in which we are told that *the glory of the Lord filled the tabernacle*,[1] and the *cloud* dwelt (*shakan*) over it. The glory of the Lord, conceived of as a bright shining cloud, was the sign of the divine presence or indwelling. Thus the ideas of God's 'glory' and of His 'indwelling' are very closely connected; one was the earnest of the other, and ultimately they became identified. But inasmuch as this *sign* of the presence of God was conceived of as something concrete, i.e. a cloud, it was in a certain sense differentiated from God Himself. This it was which in the speculations of later days gave a handle to the idea that the *medium* of God's indwelling partook of the nature of personality. It was, of course, a long process whereby the evolution of the idea ultimately reached its final

[1] The Hebrew word for tabernacle is *Mishkan*, and comes from the same root as *Shekhinah*; it was so called on account of its being Jahwe's "dwelling-place" on earth (see Exod. xxv. 8, xxix. 45, 46).

THE EVOLUTION OF THE MESSIANIC IDEA

form. In the earlier stages there are indications of somewhat *naïve* conceptions; thus in Exodus xxxiii. 9-10 we read: *And it came to pass, when Moses entered into the Tent, the pillar of cloud descended and stood at the door of the Tent, and spake* [1] *with Moses. And all the people saw the pillar of cloud stand at the door of the Tent: and all the people rose up and worshipped, every man at his tent door.* Other passages, such as that referred to previously (Exodus xl. 34 ff.), take a more spiritual view, and in these the idea of imputing personality or any independent action to the visible sign of God's glory is wholly absent; so that, as one would naturally expect, the evolution proceeds from materialistic to abstract conceptions." [2] In the Isaianic passage before us the "glory of Jahwe" denotes Jahwe's presence upon His dwelling-place on Mount Zion. The passage is an extremely interesting one, for it shows how that the ancient idea of Jahwe dwelling among His people on earth was beginning to cause the prophet heart-searchings. The representation of Jahwe

[1] The R.V. insertion of "the Lord" before "spake" has no equivalent in the original, and is, therefore, not justified; it is the "cloud" which is represented as speaking with Moses.

[2] Oesterley and Box, *op. cit.* pp. 191, 192; for the further history of the idea in the Targums and in later Jewish literature, see pp. 192-194 in the same work.

THE "BRANCH OF JAHWE"

here pictures Him as withdrawn from the gaze of men; they do not ascend up to Mount Zion and get instruction from Him; He is conceived of as enveloped in a cloud; men find shelter in a pavilion; they are permitted to enter the antechamber, as it were, but not to appear in the actual presence.

Quite in accordance with this gradual withdrawal of Jahwe is the mention of the *Branch of Jahwe*, which is the next point requiring consideration. The expression is a curious one, and occurs again, as still more obviously applying to the Messiah, in Jeremiah xxiii. 5, xxxiii. 15, Zechariah iii. 8, vi. 12. It comes from the root *Ṣamaḥ*, meaning "to sprout," and is usually employed in reference to plants and trees. In the present case it is possible that the idea of "posterity" is connected with it, for in this passage we also come across the Isaianic doctrine of the "Remnant" (see below); the root is certainly used in Isaiah xliv. 3, 4, Job viii. 19 (cf. Isa. vi. 13, to be referred to immediately) in reference to posterity; and this is the regular meaning of the word in the allied Phœnician tongue.[1] In Isaiah vi. 13 the "holy seed" is referred to as remaining, after the nation has been decimated, just as the seed remains in the stock of a tree that has been felled; but

[1] See the Oxford Hebrew Lexicon s.v.

although we get here the idea of a " Sprout " with which, from other passages (e.g. Jer. xxiii. 5), one might connect the Messiah who is to be of the seed of David, the context so obviously requires us to see in it a reference to a purified people that it can scarcely be regarded as referring to the Messiah. So that it is not from this passage that the idea of the "*Branch of Jahwe*" in reference to the Messiah arises. Some commentators are in favour of the view that the expression is to be understood in a literal sense, on account of the parallel clause, "fruit of the land";[1] if the "fruit of the land" refers to ordinary produce this interpretation would naturally commend itself; but if, as is here maintained, the whole passage is an adaptation of pre-existing myth-material, and the prophet is utilizing some form of the Golden Age myth, then it is a question whether some other idea does not underlie this expression, "Branch of Jahwe." It cannot be denied that in the book of Isaiah a variety of myths are referred to, quite apart from those under consideration; e.g. the "Helel"-(Helal) Myth[2] (xiv. 2) and the "Lilith"-Myth[3] (Isa. xxxiv. 14); so it is possible that we have here

[1] Driver, *Isaiah, his Life and Times*, p. 26 (undated); G. A. Smith, *The Book of Isaiah*, I. 32 (1890).

[2] See Gunkel, *Chaos* . . . p. 132.

[3] Cf. the writer's art. *The Demonology of the Old Testament*, in the *Expositor*, August, 1907, pp. 142-144.

THE "BRANCH OF JAHWE"

a covert reference to the "Tree of Life" Myth, which the prophet utilizes in order to illustrate how that a tree of Jahwe's planting would "in that day" give joy and blessing to the remnant of Israel; see the words in Genesis ii. 9: *And Jahwe God caused to grow* (it is the word from the root ṣamaḥ that is used) *out of the ground every tree that is pleasant to the sight; the tree of life also in the midst of the garden. . . .* This idea gains support when it is remembered that in later times the same myth was used to convey spiritual truth: *To him that overcometh will I give to eat of the tree of life* (Rev. ii. 7).[1] *Blessed are they that wash their robes, that they may have the right to come to the tree of life, and may enter in by the gates into the city* (xxii. 14). Moreover, a development of the idea contained in the passage (Isa. ii. 4–6)—according to the present interpretation—may perhaps be discerned in such words as: *The leaves of the tree were for the healing of the nations* (Rev. xxii. 2), especially as in the Isaianic passage the prophet refers to those who shall be called holy, *even every one that is written among the living in Jerusalem* (ver. 3).

It is not difficult to understand how the term "Branch," which is here used impersonally, should later on have come to be employed as a

[1] See further on this below, Chap. XVI.

THE EVOLUTION OF THE MESSIANIC IDEA

title of the Messiah; but the title gains in significance if, as pointed out, it had its roots in the idea of the "Tree of Life."

The next point in the passage to be considered is the Isaianic doctrine of the *Remnant*. This is not a doctrine which is peculiar to Isaiah, though it is a notable characteristic of his book; it is seen at work already in the Flood (*Mabbūl*) Story, and that not only in its Hebrew form. Its origin is perhaps to be looked for in the idea that prior to the coming again of a "Golden Age" all the incongruous elements which had come into the world since the original "Golden Age" would have to be obliterated; this idea must, when one thinks of it, necessarily have been a concomitant of the belief in a happy time to come, since the existence of this belief was in great part due to the circumstances in which most men found themselves. Therefore some sort of a belief in a doctrine of the *Remnant* was part of the current pre-existing material which the prophets make use of; but they greatly elevate it, and put it to a wholly spiritual use. Thus already Amos says: *As the shepherd rescueth out of the mouth of the lion two legs, or a piece of an ear; so shall the children of Israel be rescued....* (iii. 12); the reason of this destruction of the nation, bordering on total annihilation, is its wickedness: *For they know not to do right, saith Jahwe, who store*

THE "REMNANT"

up violence and robbery in their palaces (iii. 10); *Because they have sold the righteous for silver, and the needy for a pair of shoes* . . . (ii. 6–8), and often similar words occur. This doctrine of the *Remnant*, however, finds its fullest expression in the book of Isaiah, see, e.g., vi. 13, vii. 3, x. 20–23, xi. 11–16, xxviii. 1–13, and others of a like nature. The teaching contained in passages of this kind is, very briefly, as follows: The fact that the children of Israel had been chosen by God for the fulfilment of His purpose of revelation entailed responsibilities which the people at large did not recognize. It had been in vain that prophets like Amos had proclaimed: *You only have I known of all the families of the earth, therefore I will visit upon you all your iniquities* (iii. 2); the essence of the prophetical teaching had consisted not only in the Oneness of God, in contradistinction to the gods of the heathen, but also in His ethical character. Amos had taught not only: *Seek ye me, and ye shall live: but seek not Bethel, nor enter into Gilgal, and pass not to Beersheba* (Amos v. 5); but also: *Seek good, and not evil, that ye may live, and so the Lord, the God of hosts, shall be with you, as ye say: hate the evil, and love the good, and establish judgment in the gate; it may be that the Lord, the God of hosts, will be gracious unto the remnant of Joseph* (Amos v. 15). The people, on the other hand, believed that faithfulness to Jahwe

THE EVOLUTION OF THE MESSIANIC IDEA

consisted merely in the observance of prescribed forms of worship; the moral law was ignored by them. For years the prophets had taught—in vain; at length, they, Israel's *real* spiritual leaders understood that if ever Israel was to be a "people of God," a people after God's own heart, it must be a purified Israel; all the dross must be purged away, so that only the pure metal might remain. Therefore Isaiah taught the doctrine of the elect remnant, and proclaimed to them that Babylon would be the "refining-pot" (cf. the whole of Isa. xiii. with xiv. 1, 2). This was the first step in the adaptation; a second one followed with the growing conceptions of the Messianic Era, of which the passage before us contains unmistakeable, if vague, foreshadowings. The prophet could not contemplate the advent of this Era until a cleansed and purified (in a spiritual sense) people, though but a remnant, should have proved themselves fit to be the subjects of the Messianic Ruler (see further below). This is exemplified in the passage under consideration, that "day," of which the prophet speaks, will not come, i.e. the Era cannot be inaugurated, until Jahwe *shall have washed away the filth of the daughters of Zion, and shall have purged the blood of Jerusalem from the midst of her, with the spirit of judgment, and with the spirit of burning.*

This doctrine of the *Remnant* is therefore an

ISAIAH IX. 5, 6

integral part of the elements, though among the later ones, that are contained in the phrase the "Messianic Idea"; it will come before us again in dealing with the next Isaianic passage.

Isaiah ix. 5, 6 (6, 7, E.V.). *For unto us a Child is born, unto us a Son is given; and the government shall be upon his shoulder: and his name shall be called Wonderful, Counsellor, Mighty God, Everlasting Father, Prince of Peace. Of the increase of his government and of peace there shall be no end, upon the throne of David, and upon his kingdom, to establish it, and to uphold it with judgment and with righteousness from henceforth even for ever. The zeal of the Lord of hosts shall perform this.*

The central thought of the passage, ix. 1–7, which culminates in the verses above, is that of the advent of the Messiah and His kingdom because the king and the nation have proved themselves unworthy.

The first thing that must be taken note of here is that to a large extent *historical conditions* form the background of the Messianic teaching. The prophet foretells the dire calamities that are shortly to overwhelm the land:

THE EVOLUTION OF THE MESSIANIC IDEA

Behold the Lord bringeth up upon them the waters of the River, strong and many, even the king of Assyria and all his glory: and he shall come up over all his channels, and go over all his banks: and he shall sweep onward into Judah; he shall overflow and pass through; he shall reach even to the neck; and the stretching out of his wings shall fill the breadth of thy land, O Immanuel (viii. 7, 8). The small band of faithful disciples (viii. 16–18), the "remnant" in the land, are "signs and wonders" in Israel, i.e., objects of scorn, for the bulk of the people have forsaken God in their fear of the coming disaster; they have turned to their familiar spirits, to wizards, and to the spirits of the dead to succour them (viii. 19, 20); and the result of it all, in the words of the prophet, is this: *They shall look unto the earth, and behold distress and darkness, the gloom of anguish; and into thick darkness they shall be driven away* (viii. 22). It is a dark background; the more bright is the vision of the future that the prophet sees; for the faithful remnant there are words of hope: *The people that walked in darkness have seen a great light: they that dwelt in the land of the shadow of death, upon them hath the light shined* (ix. 2, in the Hebrew ix. 1). These words of hope reach their culmination in the verses (6, 7) which tell of what this light is.

It will, therefore, be seen that the prophet's Messianic teaching here finds a point of contact in the historical conditions of the time.

CHAPTER XV.

THE MESSIAH (CONTINUED).

"WONDERFUL-COUNSELLOR"—"Mighty-God"—
"Father-Everlasting"—"Prince-of-Peace"—Messianic Teaching in pre-Christian times reaches its zenith in the book of Isaiah—Isa. xi. 1–5—The outpouring of the Divine Spirit—Summary of the Isaianic teaching.

[LITERATURE :—As indicated in the footnotes.]

THE names in Is. ix. 6 which are given to the "Child" that has been born, are very striking, and need a little detailed examination, for they have an important bearing on the development of the conceptions concerning the personality of the Messiah.

Wonderful-Counsellor. Literally rendered this should be "Wonder of a Counsellor" (*Pele' Yō'ēṣ*). Obviously two conceptions are expressed here; regarding the former, a noun, it is interesting to note its Old Testament use. It is almost exclusively used in poetry, the two exceptions are Daniel xii. 6, and the verse under consideration; but more important is the fact that it is only used of *divine wonders*, it is a word that always connotes the action of God, e.g., Exodus

"WONDERFUL-COUNSELLOR"

xv. 11, Isaiah xxv. 1, Psalms lxxvii. 11, 14, lxxviii. 12, lxxxviii. 10, 12, lxxxix. 6, cxix. 129; another interesting point about the use of this word is that, with three exceptions, it always occurs in the singular number, and always in connexion with some "wonder" which God accomplished among or on behalf of the Israelites.[1] It thus becomes almost a technical term for divine interposition of a special kind in the history of His people. It is clear, therefore, that its use here is of marked significance. Concerning the second half of this title, "Counsellor," or "Adviser," there is nothing especially noteworthy in the actual word, as it is used in many connexions; but the underlying conception (remembering that it applies to the Messianic *King*) is perhaps significant in view of the early ideas concerning the duties of kingship. The etymology of the word *Melekh* ("King") connects it with the Assyrian *malâku* and the Aramaic *m'lak*,[2] which mean "to counsel"; this is well illustrated in Micah iv. 9: *Is there no king (melekh) in thee, is thy counsellor (Yō'ēṣ) perished?* Here the two words are used synonymously; the king, that is to say, is he to whom the people come for advice.

[1] An exception is Psalm lxxxviii. 11, 13, but this psalm is of an especially individualistic character.

[2] See the *Oxford Hebrew Lexicon*, p. 572b.

So that, in our passage, " Counsellor " is most likely to be understood in the sense of " Ruler," which accords well with what follows in the next verse : *Of the increase of his government and of peace there shall be no end, upon the throne of David, and upon his kingdom.*

Mighty-God. Literally " Hero-God " (*'El Gibbōr*). Here again two conceptions coalesce. The *origin* of the meaning of *'El* is doubtful ; many theories have been put forward as to what the root-idea is ; [1] but for our present purpose this is not a question of vital importance, because we are concerned with the *Old Testament* conception ; a study of its use here makes it plain that there is a good deal of justification for deriving *'El* from the root *'ūl*, " to be strong." The word is common to all Semitic races, either in the form *El* or *Il* ; this wide prevalence of the term denotes a very high antiquity, and therefore that explanation of it which is the simplest would naturally commend itself, for it is obvious that the further back we go the simpler will the conception be. Conceptions of a complex character imply a relatively high state of civilization, but it is certain that the nomads of the Arabian peninsula (the primeval home of the Semitic race) [2]

[1] See Spurrell's *Hebrew Text of Genesis*, App. II.
[2] See Winckler in *Der alte Orient* I. 10. Weber, *ibid.* III. 3.

"MIGHTY-GOD"

enjoyed a civilization of a very primitive kind. Lagarde's theory, therefore, though very attractive, is untenable; he held that *El* denoted God as "the goal of all human yearning and all human striving;"[1] this would be conceivable, nay probable, if the name *El* had been used for the first time in the prophetical period, when a pure monotheism was first enunciated, but when one remembers that the early Semites had tribal gods, and that the power of these gods was by no means conceived of as uniform, when one remembers, moreover, that the worship of these gods was to a large extent based upon ideas of utilitarianism, it becomes obvious that the conception of *El* as being "the goal of all human yearning" is one which is far too advanced. We must look for a simpler explanation. The following passages will make it clear that the word *'El* connotes the idea of strength :—Genesis xxxi. 29: *It is in the power of my hand to do evil with you*, lit. "There is to the god (*'El*) of my hand. . . ." Here the idea of "power" or "strength" in the word is very clear. 2 Kings xxiv. 15, *And they carried away captive . . . the gods of the land;* there is an ambiguity here with regard to the word "gods," the text differs from the *Q^eri*; it is perhaps not a hazardous conjecture to suppose that the original reading

[1] *Orientalia*, II. 3.

was the same as in Ezekiel xvii. 13, where the context would justify the rendering "gods" rather than "the mighty" of the Revised Version. However this may be, as the word occurs in conjunction with "officers," the *meaning* must be "mighty ones," whatever translation is given, and this is the point here insisted upon. Again, there is an especially interesting passage (Ezek. xxxii. 21) which contains the plural form of the title of the Messiah which we are examining; it runs: *And the strong ones of the mighty* (lit. " the gods of the mighty ") *shall speak to him from the midst of Sheol with them that help him.* Here again *'El* is directly connected with the idea of strength, or power, and the plural form of the very title under discussion enhances its significance.

> It is also interesting to note, in this connexion, the various meanings attaching, according to the context, to the word *'ayil*, the derivative of the root *'ûl*, viz. : " power," " hero," " oak," " ram," " pilaster " (see Exod. xv. 15 ; Ezek. xl. 9 ff., xxxi. 11 ; Isa. i. 29, lxi. 3 ; Gen. xv. 9, xxii. 13 ; 1 Kings vi. 31), all of which contain the idea of strength.

These are but a very few of a large number of passages that could be cited. But they are sufficient to show that the root ideas of *El* are " strength," and that which always goes with

MIGHTY-GOD"

strength,—" power." According to Wellhausen: "The true content of the conception of 'God' amongst the Semites generally is that of lordship";[1] to the early Semite " lordship " naturally implied strength and power.

Regarding the second half of this Messianic title," Mighty Man " (*Gibbōr*), there is no difficulty; its meaning is perfectly clear, as a few examples will show. The mythical offspring of the " Sons of God " are said to be " mighty men " (*Gibbōrim*); Nimrod is a " mighty one," or " hero," in the earth; the " man of war " and the " mighty man" are synonymous; Saul and Jonathan are called " mighty men " (see Gen. vi. 4, x. 8; 2 Sam. i. 27; Isa. iii. 2; Ezek. xxxii. 12); then there is the oft-recurring phrase, " mighty man of valour," which fully corresponds to " hero " see, e.g., Judges vi. 12, of Gideon; 1 Sam. xvi. 18, of David; 1 Kings xi. 28, of Jeroboam, etc., etc.

The meaning therefore of this second Messianic title, " Hero-God," seems to imply the conception of the semi-divine; the two parts of it appear to intimate so clearly divine strength and human strength, that one is justified in seeing in it this idea of God-Man; *not*, be it said, as yet in the Christian sense of the word, but containing the *germ* of what later revelation showed to be

[1] *Skizzen*, III. 169.

an eternal truth. If this is so, then we must see in this second title an upward step; for, while the first implied that this " Son " was to be a man, though a wonderful one, pure and simple, the second title represents him as a divine hero.

Father-Everlasting (*'Abi-'ad*). [1] Again two conceptions have to be considered in order to realize the significance of this title; and, as in the case of *Yō'ēṣ* (" Counsellor ") it is not in the actual words, but in their underlying conceptions, applied to the Messiah, that their significance lies. That the title implies *divinity* admits of no doubt; we shall come back to this presently. We have to consider, first, the general idea of Divine Fatherhood among the Israelites. Originally, among all early races gods are regarded as " fathers " after a *physical* manner; this seems to be implied in some passages in the Old Testament, e.g., in Numbers xxi. 29, Chemosh is referred to as having the Moabites as children: *He hath given his sons as fugitives, and his daughters into captivity* [2] (see also Jer. ii. 27, Mal. ii. 11); the

[1] On the formation of names compounded with *'Ab* see Buchanan Gray, *Studies in Hebrew Proper Names*, pp. 22 ff.; Lagrange, *Études sur les Religions Semitiques*, pp. 110, 111.

[2] See further, on the whole subject, Rob. Smith, *op. cit.* pp. 40 ff. (but another side of the question should also be considered, and is dealt with in the same writer's

DIVINE FATHERHOOD

curious myth referred to in Genesis vi. 4 is worth considering in this connexion; and the *suggestion* of physical fatherhood is certainly present in Exod. iv. 22, 23. But among the Hebrews the idea became spiritualized, and the idea of divine fatherhood became entirely " dissociated from the physical basis of natural fatherhood. Man was created in the image of God, but he was not begotten; God-sonship is not a thing of nature but a thing of grace. In the Old Testament, Israel is Jehovah's son, and Jehovah is his Father Who created him (*When Israel was a child, then I loved him, and called my son out of Egypt,* Hos. xi. 1; . . . *Is not he thy father that hath bought thee?* Deut. xxxii. 6); but this creation is not a physical act, it refers to the series of gracious deeds by which Israel was shaped into a nation. And so though it may be said of the Israelites as a whole, *Ye are the children of Jehovah your God* (Deut. xiv. 1), this sonship is national, not personal, and the individual Israelite has not the right to call himself Jehovah's son." [1] Now, the characteristics which the Israelites attributed to God as their spiritual Father are these: He regards them as His special possession, and looks after His children's interest (Deut. xxxii. 6 ff.);

Kinship (2nd ed.) . . . pp. 140 ff.); Stade, *Geschichte des Volkes Israel* i. 391 ff.; Lagrange, *op. cit.* pp. 110–118, where some interesting parallels will be found.

[1] Rob. Smith, *op. cit.* p. 40.

THE EVOLUTION OF THE MESSIANIC IDEA

He is the " Father of the fatherless " (Ps. lxviii. 6), shows pity (Ps. ciii. 13), is their Redeemer (Isa. lxiii. 16) and Corrector (Isa. lxiv. 7), is their Companion, or Guide, and does not retain His just anger (Jer. iii. 4), and is constantly showing them His loving-kindness (Jer. iii. 19, xxxi. 4). But of greater significance are those passages which speak of God as the Father of the nation as represented by the Davidic line ; in 2 Samuel vii. 13-16, for instance, there are, besides the conception of Divine Fatherhood, some distinct points of contact with the passage under consideration (Isa. ix. 6, 7) : . . . *I will establish the throne of his kingdom for ever. I will be his father, and he shall be my son . . . but my mercy shall not depart from him . . . . And thy house and thy kingdom shall be made sure for ever before thee : thy throne shall be established for ever*. In Psalm lxxxix. 19-37, again, all these thoughts are elaborated ; the eternal duration of the kingdom (v. 29), the divine Fatherhood (vv. 26, 27), mercy after correction (vv. 30-33), and the establishment of the throne for ever (vv. 36, 37).

These passages help us to realize the thoughts in the mind of the prophet when he applied this title of *Father-Everlasting* to the Messiah.

The second part of the title, " Everlasting " (*'ad*), witnesses to the conception of divinity which the former half bears ; it is a word, it is true, which

" PRINCE-OF-PEACE "

is by no means always used in reference to God ; but it contains the idea of " non-ending," and although many things are thus spoken of in the Old Testament, they are usually, in these cases, hyperboles ; [1] in the literal sense of " without end " it is used, as a rule, only in reference to God ; thus, of divine existence (Isa. lvii. 15), of divine attributes (Ps. cxi. 3, 10), and of the relations between God and His people (Isa. lxiv. 8 ; Mic. vii. 18), of trusting in God (Isa. xxvi. 4). [2]

> The interpretation of this title given by some scholars : " Father (i.e., distributor) of booty " (taking *'ad* in its secondary meaning), does not commend itself ; in the first place, it only occurs three times in the Old Testament with this meaning, and in two of these cases (Isa. xxxiii. 23 ; Zeph. iii. 8) the Hebrew text is not to be relied upon ; and in the second place, the passage itself forbids such an interpretation ; the words " Prince of Peace " and " Of the increase of His government and of peace there shall be no end," make the idea of " booty " very incongruous. The preceding verses, 3–5, have, truly enough, a warlike ring, but it is just the very contrast of this that vv. 6, 7 are intended to emphasize.

We must therefore see in this third title a further step, which, in a certain sense, identifies the Messiah with God ; [3] it forms the climax in the ascending scale.

[1] E.g., Psalm xxi. 6 ; Job xix. 24 ; Prov. xxix. 14.
[2] See further the *Oxford Hebrew Lexicon*, p. 723b.
[3] But cf., as against this, G. A. Smith, *Isaiah* I, p. 140.

THE EVOLUTION OF THE MESSIANIC IDEA

Prince-of-Peace (*śar-shālōm*). The normal use of שׂר (*śar*) is that of a prince under one mightier than himself (Num. xxii. 8; Amos ii. 3; Hos. iii. 4, v. 10, etc.), though in its earlier use it refers sometimes to an independent chieftain; David, for example, is spoken of as becoming "captain" (*śar*) over the four hundred malcontents who came to him in the "Cave of Adullam" (1 Sam. xxii. 2, and cf. 2 Sam. iv. 2, of Baanah and Rechab; 1 Kings ii. 24, of Rezon, son of Eliada). The significance of this title lies in the two facts that the use of *śar* indubitably points to an earthly prince, and, moreover, generally speaking, to one who is the vassal, or at all events the representative, of a king; and secondly, that it sounds the note of one of the great and distinctive characteristics of the Messianic ruler, namely that he will be a peaceful ruler (see further on this below).

The significance of these titles, therefore, seems to lie in the fact that they point to a stage in the adaptation and development of Messianic conceptions in which some of the attributes of Jahwe are being *transferred* to a personality of subordinate rank. We have seen reason above for the belief that the characteristics of a "Heilbringer" were associated with Jahwe in some of the earlier conceptions regarding Him; the brief examination above, of the titles applied to the "Child" that was to be born, show that two

"IMMANUEL"

of them, at any rate, express " Heilbringer" conceptions of the clearest kind; *'El Gibbōr*, " Hero-God," is, one might almost say, a synonym for " Heilbringer," and the Old Testament ideas connected with the two words *'El* and *Gibbōr* entirely agree with the usual representations of the " Heilbringer." To a large extent the same may be said of *'Abi-'ad*, though here, as already remarked, the idea contained in *'ad* implies an attribute which, properly speaking, can only be applied to deity. The title which, as it were, leaves the thought of a divinity behind altogether, is the last (*śar-shālōm*); though even here it is quite possible that there was in the prophet's mind the thought of the ruler during the mythic " Golden Age " of tradition ; for one of the main characteristics of this Age, in all the various forms in which it is represented, is that of peace ; moreover, as the prophet is, as already remarked, clearly in process of transferring the attributes of Jahwe to this subordinate personality, this characteristic of peace would of necessity find a place here ; for in an earlier passage, in which only Jahwe is mentioned (Isa. ii. 2-4), there is special emphasis laid on the peaceful character of the Era to come when *Jahwe* will be the ruler. But although such thoughts were, probably, in the mind of the prophet, his object evidently was to lay stress on the *human* side of this ideal ruler.

THE EVOLUTION OF THE MESSIANIC IDEA

And here it is necessary to touch in the briefest possible way upon the "Immanuel" passage (Isa. vii. 14). That in the prophet's mind the figure of Immanuel had anything to do with the Messiah, at first, seems highly improbable; it is for this reason that this passage is not dealt with in detail here; but what does seem probable is that the Immanuel-idea formed the link between Jahwe and the Prince of Peace; this will be again referred to almost immediately. Immanuel is the name given to one who is purely human, but his birth was to be the "sign" of God's power among His people (i.e., the end of the Syro-Ephraimite invasion, see vii. 1 ff.); this Immanuel-idea thus forms the point of attachment for the prophet in his purpose of presenting a human personality with (some of) the attributes of Jahwe. The human character of this ruler is emphasized in the following verse of our passage (ix. 7): *Of the increase of his government and of peace there shall be no end.* But a point of the greatest importance regarding the development of Messianic thought is the direct assertion that the ruler will sit on the throne of David. Hitherto, in the Isaianic teaching, there has been no reference to the personality of the Messiah as such; in the first passage (Isa. ii. 2-4), which lays such emphasis on the *pacific* character of the Era to come, there is, as we have seen, no reference at all to an

"IMMANUEL"

earthly ruler, it is Jahwe Himself Who reigns, in spiritual presence; and His *régime*, which is to bring peace on earth, is administered from Zion, but by means of the " law " and the " word of Jahwe." The passage is idealistic, and perhaps just for that reason, vague; it is the dream of a visionary with sublime aspirations, who has not yet got sufficiently into touch with the every-day life of men. The distinct developments noticeable in the next passage (iv. 2–6), namely that it is only a *purified* Israel that shall have their part in the happy time to come, testifies to the fact that the prophet had come face to face with the grim realities of the nation's life; but, though one may see an adumbration of a personality in the " Sprout-of-Jahwe," there is still no reference to an earthly ruler; Zion is again the centre of government, and the presence there of Jahwe is typified by the picture of " a cloud and smoke by day, and the shining of a flaming fire by night "; yet, as far as a Messianic personality is concerned, the passage is again vague. It is only when we come to the Immanuel passage (vii. 14) that there is direct mention of a human personality, Immanuel; but in this passage there is no thought of a time of peace and happiness, the Messianic Era is not even hinted at; moreover, taking the passage by itself, there is no justification for believing that in the prophet's mind, at

THE EVOLUTION OF THE MESSIANIC IDEA

the time of speaking, there was any connexion between Immanuel and a Messianic ruler. The point of importance then, here, as regards the development of Messianic thought, is that the prophet has produced a conception which would naturally form the link which was required between the kingship of Jahwe, as taught in ii. 2-4, iv. 2-6, and the ruler during the reign of peace depicted in these passages; the conception, namely, of a purely human figure upon whom, as his name shows, the spirit of Jahwe rested in a peculiarly intensive way. Now, it is the gathering up, as it were, of these conceptions, partial and to some extent immature as they are, that is presented in the passage before us (ix. 6, 7). The Immanuel-conception finds its development in the far fuller conceptions contained in the titles which are given to the child that is born; the purely human figure of vii. 14 is developed into One Who is Divine-Human; the hitherto vague conceptions of Jahwe's rule from Zion are developed into definite characteristics, " Judgment " and " Righteousness "; the earthly ruler, whose personality was before, at most, adumbrated, is now stated clearly to be one who shall sit upon the throne of David, and his rule is to be one of incessant growth, *of the increase of his government and of peace there shall be no end*, and it is to last *henceforth even for ever*.

"UNIVERSALISM" OF ISAIAH II. 2-4

With this concrete Personality and these definite characteristics of His rule, we reach a stage which, in one direction, is final; the remaining Isaianic passages do, indeed, add to the completeness of the picture here presented, but they do not add anything to the fundamental conception which has been reached. In Deutero-Isaiah there is a wholly different set of conceptions, which deal with other characteristics of the Messianic king; they develop a different side of the subject, but they can add nothing to the great outstanding conceptions of a Messianic king, Who is Divine-Human, Who is of the line of David, Who rules with judgment and in righteousness, and Whose reign is to be for ever.

In one respect, however, this passage must strike one as wanting, and it is the same with the two preceding passages (iv. 2-6, vii. 14); in all three there is no trace of that "Universalism" which is so fine and striking a characteristic of Isaiah ii. 2-4 (Mic. iv. 1-3). This omission is, however, not difficult to explain; the historical conditions of the time are fully sufficient to account for this narrowing of the prophet's horizon; Syria, Egypt and Assyria cannot, in those days, have appeared to the prophet as being fit to receive, in common with Judah, the blessings of the Messianic kingdom, which was evidently conceived of as coming in the not very far-off future.

THE EVOLUTION OF THE MESSIANIC IDEA

These are merely examples of a common element in the further development of the Messianic Idea, a development which is conditioned by the varying historical circumstances of the times. The point is merely noted here, for it is not one with which our present investigation is concerned. But there is, probably, another reason why the difference between Isaiah ii. 2-4 and iv. 2-6, vii. 14, ix. 6, 7 in the particulars indicated above, should be in evidence; ii. 2-4 is the first passage, in chronological order, in the book of Isaiah wherein the prophet makes use of the floating myth-material to which reference has been made above; the absence, therefore, of " particularistic " ideas is a very natural feature of the passage; but having once incorporated this material into his teaching, it was inevitable that the prophet should, in his subsequent use of it, colour it and adapt it in accordance with the new mental atmosphere into which it had been transported; and therefore, in the later " Messianic " passages the impress of what was not an original element in the material utilized, makes itself evident. It is interesting to observe that in Micah iv. 1-3, where almost the identical words of Isaiah ii. 2-4 reappear, the passage continues: *But they shall sit every man under his vine and under his fig-tree; and none shall make them afraid;* a fact which suggests that the Isaianic passage is

ISAIAH XI. 1-5

presented in an incomplete form. That Micah was less discriminating than Isaiah in the use that each made of earlier material is perhaps evidenced by the fact that he adds some words which, in the mouth of an eighth century prophet, sound somewhat strange: *For all the peoples will walk every man in the name of his god, and we will walk in the name of Jahwe our God, for ever and ever.*

Isaiah xi. 1-5: *And there shall come forth a twig out of the trunk of Jesse, and a branch out of his roots shall shoot up* (cf. the Septuagint and the Vulgate);

And the spirit of Jahwe shall rest upon him; the spirit of wisdom and discernment;

The spirit of counsel and power, the spirit of knowledge and fear of Jahwe, yea, the spirit of the fear of Jahwe shall fill him (cf. the Septuagint and the Vulgate).

Not according to what his eyes see shall he judge, and not according to what his ears hear shall he decide;

But he shall judge the poor with righteousness, and shall decide on behalf of the downcast of the land with uprightness.

And he shall smite him that causeth terror (reading *'ariṣ*),[1] *with the rod of his mouth, and with the breath of his lips shall he slay the wicked.*

[1] Most authorities, from Gesenius onwards, read this instead of *'ereṣ* ("earth"); the reading *'ereṣ* does not give good sense, both the context (in 4a) and the *parallelismus membrorum* require (in 4b) the emendation as suggested above.

THE EVOLUTION OF THE MESSIANIC IDEA

And righteousness shall be the girdle[1] *of (around) his hips, and faithfulness the waist-cloth*[1] *of his loins.*

Verses 6-9, which belong to this passage, will be considered later on, as they will come more appropriately in the chapter on the Messianic Era.

The thought underlying the use of the words *ḥōṭĕr* and *neṣer* must be the same as in the case of *ṣemaḥ*, spoken of above. There is no ambiguity as to the meaning of the words, referring as they do to the growth of trees or plants; but they are rare ones, occurring only a few times in the Old Testament, e.g., *neṣer* is used of the people of Judah in Isaiah xvi. 21, and Babylon is spoken of as a " rotten branch " (assuming that the reading *neṣer* is correct) in Isaiah xiv. 19; *ḥōṭĕr* only occurs once elsewhere (Prov. xiv. 3); the difference in meaning between the two words is simply that *neṣer* is what *ḥōṭĕr* develops into.

The words, *And the spirit of Jahwe shall rest upon him*, require a little closer attention, as the idea they express forms a not unimportant element in the development of the Messianic Idea. The two expressions, " Spirit of Jahwe " and " Spirit of God " (*'Elohim*) seem, at all events in the earlier literature, to be used indiscriminately, cf. e.g. such passages as Numbers xi. 17, 1 Samuel x. 6 with

[1] *'Azôr* in 5a should perhaps be emended to *ḥăgôr* as it is contrary to the general usage to have the identical word in each half of the verse.

THE SPIRIT OF JAHWE

1 Samuel x. 10, xix. 20, etc.; so that no significance can be attached to the Septuagint rendering "Spirit of God." Moreover, not only a good spirit, as in the passages just referred to, but evil spirits are also spoken of as coming from Jahwe, or from God, e.g. "Spirit of Jahwe," 1 Samuel xvi. 14, xix. 9, 1 Kings xxii. 21, 22, and "Spirit of God," 1 Samuel xvi. 15, xviii. 10. In the earlier times the spirit of Jahwe, or of God, was almost invariably connected with the ecstatic state of "prophets" (*Nĕbī'īm*, including under this term *rō'eh* and *hōzeh*, as well as *nabī'*), whether good or bad. Amos repudiates all relationship with the *Nebī'īm*, "Prophets" (vii. 14, though comp. iii. 7); but a marked difference was taking place from the period of Amos onwards—perhaps owing mainly to his "prophetical" activity—for although, in the time of Hosea, we find the people in general still looking upon the prophets with contempt (Hos. ix. 7), yet he himself does not repudiate the title (ver. 8), and in vi. 5, xii. 10, 13, the prophetical office is honoured. Isaiah speaks of the taking away of the prophets as a calamity for the land (iii. 1 ff.), though he recognizes that, like the priests, they are not always guiltless (ix. 15, xxviii. 7, xxix. 10). It would seem, therefore, that concurrently with this more honourable position which the prophetic office was assuming, there was also a developing process

going on in the conceptions concerning the action of the spirit of Jahwe upon men. And this is quite in accordance with what one would expect, for the period preceding that of the age of Isaiah had seen the rise of a new order of prophets, the spirit of whose teaching was immensely in advance of what had gone before. Therefore, when Isaiah spoke of the " spirit of Jahwe " resting upon a man, it must have connoted something very different from that of the similar phrase in earlier passages ; but, as in the earlier passages— and this is the point of importance here—it had reference to a prophet, i.e. a *man*, and in the passage before us that man is the Messiah ; so that, according to the teaching here, the Messiah was to be a *prophet*, of the stem or " trunk " of Jesse (cf. Deut. xviii. 15). This was an entirely new conception concerning the functions of the Messiah ; for he has now become, according to the Isaianic teaching on the subject, a great prophet of Judah, differing from other prophets who had gone before only in the more abundant outpouring upon him of the spirit of Jahwe.

The term which is here used for describing the influence of the spirit of Jahwe upon the Messiah that is to come, is *nūaḥ* ; as used in this connexion the word is extremely rare, occurring elsewhere only in Numbers xi. 25, 26 ; other expressions used in connexion with *rūaḥ* (" spirit ") not necessarily

THE SPIRIT OF JAHWE

the divine spirit, are *śūm* (" to put "), Numbers xi. 17; *hayah* (" to be "), Judges iii. 10, xi. 29 and often; *nasak* (" to pour out "), Isaiah xxix. 10; *nathan* (" to give "), Isaiah xlii. 1, Ezekiel xi. 19; *yaṣaq* (" to pour "), Isaiah xliv. 3 and others; almost invariably in these cases *ruah* is a feminine noun (it is always so when used of the spirit of God, in the Old Testament), which, as being equivalent to the neuter, precludes the idea of personality being attributed to it; though in some of the references given above, the action might almost imply the idea of personality (cf. further Isa. lxiii. 10, 11). This is interesting in view of the later Jewish doctrine of the Holy Spirit.[1]

But the fulness of the outpouring of the divine spirit is clearly intended, by the prophet's description, to be unique in its character; and the details of the Messianic personality, here portrayed, supplement, as far as the purely human attributes are concerned, the description in Isaiah ix. 6, 7. As this represents the final stage of the Isaianic conceptions of the Messiah, and as these strongly influenced subsequent teaching on the subject, it may be well to examine briefly the details of the prophet's description.

[1] On this subject see Oesterley and Box, *op. cit*, pp. 84-91.

THE EVOLUTION OF THE MESSIANIC IDEA

The spirit of wisdom and discernment ; the idea of this combination of wisdom and discernment is found in other passages, viz. in I Kings v. 9 of the wisdom of Solomon ; in I Kings vii. 14 of the skill in brass-working on the part of the artificer, Hiram ; in Isaiah x. 13, where the Assyrian king ascribes his victories to his own wisdom and prudence ; and in Isaiah xxix. 14, where, it is said, *the wisdom of their wise men shall perish, and the understanding of their prudent men shall be hid.* These passages go to show that the nature of the wisdom and discernment of which the prophet was thinking when he attributed them to the coming Messiah, was not other than that of which any man might be possessed. In accordance, therefore, with the earlier part of this passage, in which the coming Messiah is represented as one who would be a descendant of Jesse, the prophet does not claim for him anything which does not belong to humanity in general ; the differentiation between this figure and other men lies in the more abundant outpouring of Jahwe's spirit upon him, which is evidenced by the phrases that follow.

The spirit of counsel and power ; this phrase does not call for special remark ; it emphasizes what has just been said. Both words, " counsel " as well as " power," are used of God as well as of men in the book of Isaiah and elsewhere ; the words are used together in reference to expertness

THE SPIRIT OF JAHWE

in warfare in Isaiah xxxvi. 5 (and in the parallel passage, 2 Kings xviii. 20).

The spirit of knowledge and the fear of Jahwe; " Knowledge " (*da'ath*) stands closely connected with *hokmah* (" wisdom ") and *binah* (" understanding "), not infrequently all three appear in close relationship, e.g. Isaiah xl. 14,[1] Proverbs ii. 6, Job x. 7, Psalm cxxxix. 6, Proverbs iii. 20 (in the last three passages in reference to God). " Fear of Jahwe " is a fairly common expression belonging almost exclusively to the later literature. Emphasis is laid upon the Messiah's characteristic of " judging " (*shaphat*); this is of particular interest and importance, for it was herein that the main activity of the king consisted in times of peace (cf. 2 Sam. xv. 4, 1 Kings iii. 9, 2 Kings xv. 5); peacefulness is to be the pre-eminent mark of the Messianic Era (see further on this below), and therefore *shaphat* (" to judge ") is a specially characteristic word in the Isaianic texts concerning the Messiah and the Messianic Era. Very striking, as showing the development of spiritual conception, are the thoughts that the Messiah will smite with the " rod of His mouth,' and slay with the " breath of His lips." This spiritual atmosphere is further emphasized by the figurative expressions which follow; the

[1] The text of this passage is not free from suspicion, the Septuagint omits part of it.

THE EVOLUTION OF THE MESSIANIC IDEA

'ezôr was a woollen cloth which enveloped the body from the waist to the middle of the thighs, so that it did not only encircle this part of the body, but enveloped it; the idea conveyed, therefore, is that the coming Messiah will be, as it were, enclosed within righteousness and faithfulness (cf. the " whole armour of God," Eph. vi. 13, 14).

* * * * *

The four passages from the book of Isaiah which have been considered do not, of course, exhaust the Messianic texts which it contains; but they are the most important; some others, both in this book and in other books, will be incidentally referred to later on. These four, however, which (it is believed) have been dealt with in their chronological order, present us with the essence of the process of the adaptation and development of the person of the Messiah. The steps in this process are of such paramount importance for our present purpose, that it may be well to indicate them once more in as succinct a manner as possible.

In the *first* passage (ii. 2–4) Jahwe Himself is the Messianic ruler; He is to be the universal Judge over all peoples. The ruler is divine, His subjects include all nations.

In the *second* passage (iv. 2–6) Jahwe is still the Messianic ruler on earth, but His presence is

RECAPITULATION

indicated by the *Shekhinah* ; His subjects are now restricted to the purified children of Israel. A new element has entered the circle of ideas, namely the " Branch of Jahwe," forming the point of attachment for the idea of the " shoot," or " twig," of Jesse.

In the *third* passage (ix. 5, 6) a divine-human ruler—the Immanuel-conception (vii. 14) forming the link—sits upon the throne of David ; His subjects are the children of Israel.

In the *fourth* passage (xi. 1-5) a purely human ruler, upon whom the spirit of Jahwe is manifest in a unique manner, is presented ; he is a descendant of Jesse, and therefore, presumably, his subjects are restricted to the children of Israel.

It seems, therefore, incontrovertible that, if one is to take these passages as they stand, in their natural meaning, and without reading into them thoughts and ideas which belong to later ages, one is forced to the conclusion that, at first, the prophet believed in the actual, visible presence of Jahwe Himself on earth, as the ruler in the time when universal peace, righteousness and happiness should come. This conception was primarily an adaptation of the ancient belief in the return of the happy time of long ago, when the gods dwelt on earth and ruled. It is well to recall here the fact that there are many instances whereby it can be shown that in the Old

THE EVOLUTION OF THE MESSIANIC IDEA

Testament the worship of Jahwe was not the original worship of the Israelite nation, but that it displaced that of other gods, which resulted in *transferring to Jahwe* the beliefs and ideas which before had been held with regard to these other gods. One has but to remember the place that Canaanite *Baalism* occupied at one time among the Israelites, and that after allegiance had been transferred from the *Baalim* to Jahwe the actual difference of both worship and belief consisted, for long, only in holding them in relation to a God of another name, and that only by slow degrees did a true, purified Jahwe-worship come into existence,—one has but to remember these facts, in order to realize that it is only what one would naturally look for when we find the prophet taking the old, time-honoured beliefs of untold generations, and adapting them to his far higher and more spiritual teaching. But with his ever-increasing realization of the transcendent majesty and glory of God, there must have impressed itself upon him more and more the incongruousness of His actual presence among sinful men. Perhaps the first stage in the solution of this difficulty was his belief that, after a purifying process, a cleansed remnant would be found worthy of Jahwe's presence in their midst (iv. 2–6); but the real solution lay at last in his doctrine that Jahwe's *representative* would be the ruler in the

RECAPITULATION

happy time to come; upon him the spirit of Jahwe would be poured out in a way altogether unique, which would be the counterpart of Jahwe's actual presence. When once the idea of a human ruler in the happy time to come had arisen, there were special reasons for connecting him with the house of David; with these reasons we are not concerned here; it is enough to mention the fact as belonging to the process of development. But it may be added that it was probably owing to this fact that the specific name " Messiah," as applied to the ruler who was to come, arose.

The Isaianic teaching on this subject contains all the most essential points, and therefore, although much might be said in reference to it, by taking other books of the Bible into consideration, for our present purpose this is not called for, the discussion of the passages referred to being deemed sufficient.

CHAPTER XVI.

THE MESSIANIC ERA.

The meaning of the phrase " The Day of Jahwe "—The prophetical conception of this " Day " contrasted with the popular conception—Further development of ideas concerning this " Day "—Some examples of adaptation and development of the " Golden Age " myth : its peaceful character ; a time of happiness and contentment—The " Mount of God "—The " River of Life "—The " Tree of Life."

[Literature :—As indicated in the footnotes.]

As we have seen above (Chaps. X., XI.) the " Paradise-Myth,"—as its Old Testament form should be called, the " Golden Age Myth " in more general terms—consists of two complementary parts, the one referring to man in a primeval state of happiness, the other to the return of this in the distant future. The Messianic Era properly speaking, is, of course, concerned with the latter of these only. The attempt has been made, in the chapters just referred to, to show that the Israelite teachers made use of the floating material regarding this myth in order to adapt it to more spiritual teaching.

Our task is now to examine briefly the main characteristics of the Messianic Era in the light of what has been said above, and to note some of the

"THE DAY OF JAHWE"

developments which mark the Israelite treatment of the subject.

I.

The first point to deal with is the idea, or circle of ideas, contained in the phrase, "The Day of Jahwe." The first time that this phrase occurs is in Amos v. 18: "Woe unto them that desire the Day of Jahwe."[1] Here it is to be noted that the words are used as a kind of *terminus technicus*; every one among those whom the prophet is addressing, knows what he is referring to, cf. viii. 9, 13; it follows, therefore, that although the phrase occurs in Amos v. 18 for the first time, it must have been in use long before, to have become so familiar among the people as this passage leads one to suppose. It is, moreover, obvious that the people had a different conception regarding the "Day of Jahwe" from that of the prophet; the question is, which of these two conceptions (whatever their content) was the more original? On *a priori* grounds it is the popular conception which one would naturally suppose to be the older. But it will be well to examine, as far as this is possible, the respective beliefs of Amos and the people generally, concerning this "Day." That of the prophet is as

[1] It seems also, however, to be in the prophet's mind in such passages as i. 2, iii. 2*b*, 12.

THE EVOLUTION OF THE MESSIANIC IDEA

follows: In v. 17, the words: *For I will pass through the midst of thee, saith Jahwe*, evidently from the context, refer to the " Day of Jahwe "; the preceding words are: *Therefore thus saith Jahwe, the God of Hosts* (the Lord [omitted in the Septuagint]), *Wailing shall be in all the broad ways; and they shall say in all the streets, Alas! alas! and they shall call the husbandmen to mourning, and such as are skilful of lamentation to wailing. And in all vineyards shall be wailing* (v. 16, 17a); then further: *Woe unto you that desire the day of Jahwe! wherefore would ye have the day of Jahwe? it is darkness and not light. . . . Shall not the day of Jahwe be darkness and not light? even very dark, and no brightness in it?* (v. 18–20) and again: *And the songs of the temple shall be howlings in that day, saith the Lord Jahwe: the dead bodies shall be many . . .* (viii. 3); *And it shall come to pass in that day, saith the Lord Jahwe, that I will cause the sun to go down at noon, and I will darken the earth in the clear day. And I will turn your feasts into mourning, and all your songs into lamentation. . . . And they shall wander from sea to sea, and from the north even to the east; they shall run to and fro to seek the word of Jahwe, and shall not find it . . . and I will slay the last of them with the sword: there shall not one of them flee away, and there shall not one of them escape. Though they dig into Sheol, thence shall mine hand take them; and*

"THE DAY OF JAHWE"

though they climb up to heaven, thence will I bring them down. And though they hide themselves in the top of Carmel, I will search and take them out thence; and though they be hid from my sight in the bottom of the sea, thence will I command the serpent, and he shall bite them. And though they go into captivity before their enemies, thence will I command the sword, and it shall slay them: and I will set mine eyes upon them for evil, and not for good. . . . (viii. 9—ix. 8). This is the prophet's idea of the "Day of Jahwe." Now, it must be noted that from v. 18 it seems clear that the prophet is correcting what he knows to be the people's idea of this "Day"; the point of his teaching here is to show them that their idea is the very reverse of what is actually to take place. It will, therefore, not be arbitrary if we surmise that the people's idea of the "Day" was the reverse of much of what Amos says upon the subject. At all events, it is worth while to construct a picture of which the opposite of the essential points of the prophet's words forms the contents. In this case the "Day" which the people desire is approximately as follows:—The presence of Jahwe; this is self-evident, otherwise that "Day" would not be called the "Day of Jahwe," and therefore when the prophet says: *For I will pass through the midst of thee,* he touches the point of attachment between his own and the people's

THE EVOLUTION OF THE MESSIANIC IDEA

view; all believed in His actual presence in that "Day" (cf. the Isaianic conception above); the difference of view arose as to what His action would be when He should come. According to the interpretation here given the people expected, not "wailing in the street," but rejoicing; not cries of "Alas! alas!" but shouts of joy; not mourning on the part of the husbandman, nor wailing in the vineyards, but "every man sitting under his vine and under his fig-tree, for the mouth of Jahwe of hosts hath spoken it" (Mic. iv. 4); for such reasons they *desired*, as Amos says, the "Day of Jahwe." But further, the people, so far from expecting that the "Day of Jahwe" would be darkness and not light—note how the prophet lays stress on this, the interrogatory form in which it is put suggests that he is combating the popular view—believed that then they would see "the glory of Jahwe and the excellency of their God" (Isa. xxxv. 2); so far from expecting that the songs of the temple should be howlings in that day—note, again, the opposites, "songs" and "howlings"—they believed that it would be a time when they would "come with singing unto Zion," when "everlasting joy should be upon their heads," when they should "obtain gladness and joy, and sorrow and sighing should flee away" (Isa. xxxv. 10; cf. Isa. li. 3). Moreover, in the passages above, in which the prophet's

"THE DAY OF JAHWE"

views of the "Day of Jahwe" are described, there seem to be some references to antique ideas about Jahwe of which mention has been made in some earlier chapters; thus, in their search for Jahwe, the prophet says the people shall wander from the north even to the east; the fact of their going to the "north" recalls what has been said about Jahwe's Mountain being situated in the north. There is also the mention of Jahwe's "sword"; according to the popular belief this was that with which Jahwe "clave in pieces" the Dragon, and with which He would finally destroy the watery monster, lurking, as Amos says, "in the bottom of the sea." So that, without going into further details, which might easily be done by drawing attention to other passages previously dealt with, the conception of the "Day of Jahwe," as pictured in the popular imagination, seems clear enough, if the method whereby we have sought to obtain this be deemed legitimate. In any case, it is a striking coincidence that these popular ideas of the "Day of Jahwe" should so entirely agree with what we have already seen to be the characteristics of the "Golden Age Myth," constructed out of the materials which had for generations been floating among the people. Assuming, therefore, that the popular idea of the "Day of Jahwe" was actually as portrayed above, we must see in the prophet's idea of the "Day" an adaptation of what had gone before.

Professor Charles (in *Encycl. Bibl.* art. *Eschatology*), writing of the popular conception of the "Day of Jahwe" at the time of Amos, says that the Israelites "not only looked forward to, but also earnestly prayed for, the 'day of Yahwe' as the time of his vindication of them against their enemies"; he speaks also of "the primitive conception of the day of Yahwe" being "a judgment of Israel's enemies."[1] In the same way Professor G. A. Smith says: "So Jehovah's day meant to the people the day of His judgment, or of His triumph. His triumph in war over their enemies, His judgment upon the heathen."[2] That this became, later on, the popular conception of the "Day of Jahwe" admits of no doubt at all; it may, however, be questioned whether this was the "primitive conception" of the people. In the book of Amos, which contains the earliest mention of the subject, there does not seem to be sufficient evidence to justify this; moreover, the historical conditions of the time were not such as would require an expectation of this kind; the country was at the height of prosperity; its enemies had been conquered; political security was established; and the country enjoyed unparalleled wealth; Jeroboam II had, during his long reign, brought his land to a high state of prosperity. It might well have seemed to those whom the prophet was addressing—it was, of course, different with the poor—that the fabled "Golden Age" (or the equivalent Hebrew conception of it) was about to be inaugurated. If

[1] Col. 1348.
[2] *The Book of the Twelve Prophets*, I., p. 169 (1896).

"THE DAY OF JAHWE"

Amos, with prophetic vision, foresaw the approach, in the near future, of a more powerful enemy than had yet been met with during the nation's history, it is certain that the people at large had no thoughts of anything of the kind. Therefore, it does not seem probable that at this time the popular conception of the "Day of Jahwe" included the idea of Jahwe's coming to conquer their enemies. It is true that they believed that He was coming to wield a sword, but this sword was that by which He had overcome the Dragon (according to the popular myth), and it would now be used to bring about the final annihilation of the monster;[1] it will be remembered that stress has constantly been laid on the fact that the Dragon or Serpent was believed still to be in existence. From this point of view there is a special appropriateness in the prophet's allusion to the Serpent in the depths of the sea, for, according to him, Jahwe was going to command this monster to slay (bite) the evil ones among the people; the destruction of these, together with the final annihilation of the Serpent, would be the preparation for the inauguration of the Messianic Era.

We conclude, therefore, that according to the popular conception before and during the time of Amos, the "Day of Jahwe" meant the inauguration of the "Golden Age." Amos is the first to adapt this to his teaching, and in accordance

[1] It is, of course, not denied that there were other elements which contributed to the popular desire that the "Day of Jahwe" should come, e.g., local calamities such as are referred to in Amos iv. 6–11.

with his immensely advanced conceptions of the majesty and ethical purity of Jahwe, he declares that this " Day of Jahwe " will in reality prove to be a terrible exhibition of His just wrath upon all the *wicked*, whether in Israel or among the surrounding nations (cf. chaps. i., ii.), though the former are more especially the objects of His indignation, on account of the signal marks of His help and guidance which in the past they had experienced,—*You only have I known of all the families of the earth ; therefore I will visit upon you all your iniquities* (Amos iii. 2). The wicked among the surrounding nations are to be punished, not because they are the enemies of Israel, but because their wickedness marks them out as the enemies of Jahwe.

This adaptation, which the prophet Amos was the first to make use of, was further developed and elaborated by later prophets ; the most striking and oft-recurring form which this development took—though here again it was Amos who first set the key—was to indicate certain nations who were to take the place of Jahwe— or rather, to act as His instruments—in punishing Israel (or Judah, as the case might be) ; thus, e. g., Amos says : *For behold, I will raise up against you a nation, O house of Israel, saith Jahwe, the God of hosts ; and they shall afflict you from the entering in of Hamath unto the brook of the*

"THE DAY OF JAHWE"

Arabah (vi. 14). Hosea—the context shows that he is referring to some foreign foe—prophesies: *Ephraim shall become a desolation in the day of rebuke: among the tribes of Israel have I made known that which shall surely be;* so, too, Isaiah, e.g., in x. 3: *And what will ye do in the day of visitation, and in the desolation which shall come from far? To whom will ye flee for help? and where will ye leave your glory?* In connexion with this see x. 5–7: *Ho, Assyrian . . . I will send him against a profane nation, and against the people of my wrath will I give him a charge, to take the spoil, and to take the prey, and to tread them down like the mire of the streets . . . ;* cf. also Isaiah v. 25–30; Micah vii. 12, 13; Habakkuk i. 6 ff., etc., etc. While all these prophets thus explain the "Day of Jahwe" to be His visitation upon the people of Israel and Judah, through the instrumentality of foreign nations, they emphasize over and over again that these nations, too, shall be punished on account of their *wickedness*; this was the natural result of the prophetic teaching concerning the Personality of Jahwe. The most emphatic expression of this, however, is found in the book of Zephaniah, e.g., i. 4: *I will stretch out my hands upon Judah, and upon all the inhabitants of Jerusalem . . .* i. 7 ff.: *For the day of Jahwe is at hand: for Jahwe hath prepared a sacrifice,*

THE EVOLUTION OF THE MESSIANIC IDEA

he hath sanctified his " guests." And it shall come to pass in the day of Jahwe's sacrifice, that I will punish the princes, and the King's sons . . . ; the judgment is also pronounced over other nations, Philistia, Ethiopia, Assyria (ii. 1-15) ; even the brute creation is included in the destruction that shall come about in the " Day of Jahwe " (i. 2, 3). In post-exilic times a further development takes place ; the *restoration* of Israel, and the *destruction* of the Gentiles becomes more and more characteristic of the prophetic attitude, though Jeremiah (and sometimes Ezekiel, see below) forms a notable exception. We are not, however, concerned here so much with the later stages of development. Our main point is, that the " Day of Jahwe " conceived of in the first instance as the inauguration of the " Golden Age," in the popular conception, was taken over by the prophets and adapted to a different purpose ; His " Day " was indeed to come, but it would be a time of terrible visitation because of the wickedness of the people. This prophetic conception seems to have reached its fulfilment at the time of the Captivity, so that in post-exilic times the prophets, for the most part, speak of the *restoration* of the nation.

But the whole conception of the " Day of Jahwe " from the prophetic point of view implied that it was to be the vindication in the eyes of the

"THE DAY OF JAHWE"

whole world of Jahwe's character of majesty, justice and righteousness; the "Day of Jahwe" was not an end in itself, it was the means whereby the nation was to be cleansed and purified, and made fit to be the true people of Jahwe; it was the process whereby the "Messianic Era" was to become a fact. Even on the prophetic view, therefore, it was possible to look beyond this cleansing process, and contemplate the time of peaceful, happy contentment—even if enjoyed by a "Remnant" only—which should ultimately be the lot of those who were faithful to Jahwe. In other words, the *popular* conception of the return of the "Golden Age" was not altogether ignored by the prophets; this popular conception was older than the prophetic one, as we have seen, and it was a time-honoured belief held very dear, as such ancient traditions always are, more especially when they promise something bright in the future. For the prophets, therefore, to make use of this popular conception as it stood— apart from their adaptation of the "Day of Jahwe" as mentioned above—and adapt it, in the popular sense, to higher and more spiritual teaching, was entirely in accordance with what happened in the case of many other things. That the prophetical teaching and preaching should have consisted only in menace, that there should have been only denunciation and no encouragement, would have been highly improbable—on the contrary, in the prophetical writings we have ample witness to the fact that they frequently used gentle means to persuade their hearers to depart from evil, and the promises of reward for those who obeyed the voice of Jahwe are by no means isolated. If in the case of Amos this cannot be said,[1] reasons for this exception to the general rule could easily be adduced. And therefore, side by side with the prophetic conception of the " Day of Jahwe," we find another picture of a time to come, which the prophets employed for the purposes of encouragement and hope as well as for higher spiritual teaching. This picture was taken from the popular conception of the " Golden Age," and utilized by the prophets.

II.

We have seen reason to believe (Chaps. X., XI.) that the myth of the " Golden Age " was well known to the Israelites, and that some of their teachers made use of this pre-existing myth-material for the purpose of adapting it to Messianic prophecy; we must now, very briefly, examine a few examples of the adaptation and development of this—the popular—form of the time to come.

[1] Amos ix. 11–15 must undoubtedly be placed in exilic or post-exilic times.

THE MESSIANIC ERA A TIME OF PEACE

1. One of the chief characteristics of the "Golden Age," in practically every form in which it appears, is that of *peace*. Isaiah, adapting this characteristic in one of his prophecies concerning the Messianic Era, says: *They shall beat their swords into plowshares, and their spears into pruning hooks; nation shall not lift up sword against nation, neither shall they learn war any more* (ii. 4; Mic. iv. 3) ; it is very striking that all nations are included in this picture of peace; the same *trait* is found in another Isaianic passage (xi. 9), in which, moreover, a development in a different direction is noticeable: *They shall not hurt nor destroy in all my holy mountain; for the earth shall be full of the knowledge of Jahwe, as the waters cover the sea.* Here one sees that already the restricted area of the locality in which the scene is laid, viz. the mount of Jahwe, has become extended, and it is used as a parallel [1] to the "earth"; but more important is the spiritual development in that it is said that "the knowledge of Jahwe" is to be widespread in that time. To "know" Jahwe is to believe in His power, and to obey His word; the prophet therefore lifts the thoughts into a higher, a spiritual atmosphere, very different from the

---

[1] That *'ereṣ* is used here in the wider sense of the "earth," and not merely in that of the "land," i.e. of Israel, seems clear from the verse (10) which follows.

THE EVOLUTION OF THE MESSIANIC IDEA

materialistic conceptions which had been associated with the Age to come. The peace that is to reign there is not to arise from weariness of war, or because men love ease and enjoyment, but it is to be a peace which results from " knowing " Jahwe. This peaceful character is seen emphasized in the title " Prince of Peace " (Isa. ix. 6), which is given to the Messianic ruler, and in the words : *Of the increase of his government and of peace there shall be no end* (verse 7) ; but it is always a peace which is the outcome of knowing Jahwe, for the kingdom in the Messianic Era is to be established and upheld, *with judgment and with righteousness from henceforth even for ever ; the zeal of Jahwe of hosts shall perform this*. This development is, further, illustrated in Jeremiah xxiii. 5, 6 (cf. xxxiii. 14–16) : *Behold, days are coming, saith Jahwe, that I will raise to David a righteous shoot, and he shall reign as King, and will deal wisely, and he will execute judgment and righteousness in the land. In his days Judah shall be saved, and Israel* [1] *shall dwell safely ; and this is his name whereby he shall be called, " Jahwe our righteousness."* The conditions of a reign of peace are emphasized here ; judgment and righteousness, without which lasting and

[1] In the parallel passage, Jeremiah xxxiii. 16 (which is wanting in the Septuagint), the reading is " Jerusalem " instead of " Israel " ; in the passage before us the Septuagint (א) reads " Jerusalem."

THE MESSIANIC ERA A TIME OF PEACE

true peace is impossible, are strongly characteristic of the prophetic development. Another passage which must be quoted is of special interest, for in it is found a curious mixture of antique thought and more advanced ideas; one *trait*, at least, belonging to the old-world conception of the "Golden Age," is prominent, while the passage itself witnesses to quite late development; it is Ezekiel xxxiv. 20-31, but especially vv. 22-25: *Therefore will I save my flock, and they shall no more be a prey, and I will judge between sheep and sheep. And I will raise up One Shepherd for them, and he shall feed them, namely my servant David, and he shall be unto them for a shepherd. And I, Jahwe, will be their God, and David a prince in their midst; I, Jahwe, have said it. And I will make with them a covenant of peace, and I will cause evil beasts to cease from the land; that they may dwell in the wilderness, and sleep in the woods.* With this should be compared, first of all, the following more or less parallel passage (Ezek. xxxvii. 24-28): *And my servant David shall be king over them* (i.e. over the united kingdoms of Israel and Judah), *and there shall be one shepherd for them all, and they shall walk in my judgments, and shall observe my statutes to fulfil them. And they shall dwell in the land that I gave unto my servant Jacob where their fathers dwelt, even therein shall they dwell, they*

THE EVOLUTION OF THE MESSIANIC IDEA

and their children, and their children's children, for ever; and David my servant shall be their prince for ever. And I will make a covenant of peace with them, an everlasting covenant shall it be with them, and I will place my sanctuary in the midst of them for ever.[1] *And my dwelling-place shall be over them,*[2] *and I will be their God, and they shall be my people. And the nations shall know that it is I, Jahwe, who sanctifieth Israel, when my sanctuary is among them for ever.*

In the main points these two passages are parallel; but in the former occurs the antique *trait* of the removal of the wild beasts from the land in the Messianic Era; the mention of this is interesting as showing that the prophet is utilizing ancient material and adapting it to his teaching (cf. Isaiah xxxv. 9 : *No lion shall be there, nor shall any ravenous beast go up thereon, they shall not be found there*);[3] in Isaiah xi. 6–8, the idea of an alteration in the nature of the animals is presented; under such circumstances their existence during the Messianic Era is not thought

[1] Omitting, with Cornill, *And I will place them and multiply them.*

[2] Cf. Isaiah iv. 5.

[3] It is possible that the belief in a connexion, or community of interests, between animals and demons may have had something to do with the stress that is laid on the disappearance of wild beasts in the Messianic Era; see the writer's art. "The Demonology of the Old Testament," in the *Expositor*, April, 1907, pp. 329–331.

THE MESSIANIC ERA A TIME OF PEACE

incongruous. In other respects these passages forcibly illustrate the development that has taken place; the covenant of peace, and its everlasting character, walking in the judgments of Jahwe, and observing His statutes, as well as the presence of His sanctuary, all show how spiritual teaching has taken the place of the original materialistic conceptions which, as we have seen, were the characteristics of the " Golden Age," according to the popular fancies. One other passage must be referred to as showing the spiritual development of the conceptions of the Messianic Era regarding its peaceful character, viz. Zechariah ix. 9-10: *Rejoice greatly, daughter of Zion, shout, daughter of Jerusalem ; behold thy King cometh unto thee ; righteous is he and one that saves* (cf. the Septuagint), *lowly, and riding upon an ass, even upon the colt of a she-ass. And he will destroy* (cf. the Septuagint) *the chariots out of Ephraim and the horses out of Jerusalem ; and the battle bow shall be destroyed, and he shall declare peace unto the nations ; and his rule shall be from sea to sea, and from the river unto the ends of the earth.* A universal reign of peace is here prophesied ; but although this peace is described in literal language, as following upon war and tumult in the ordinary sense of the word, the thought of a different kind of peace underlies the prophet's words as well. The words, " righteous is he and one that saves "

THE EVOLUTION OF THE MESSIANIC IDEA

—following the Septuagint reading, which certainly seems to commend itself, owing to the context—herald a spiritual peace, a " peace of God," rather than a mere cessation of hostilities. What further suggests this is the character of humility in which the Messianic King is portrayed; this humility as a characteristic of the Messiah is very striking: " The riding of the Messiah upon an ass," says Gressmann, " which is here used as a sign of humility, has hitherto always been regarded as something self-understood, without its having called forth any surprise. Nowhere else, however, is the eschatological King conceived of as specially *humble-minded*, nor can the destruction of the chariots and the creation of a peaceful nation be regarded as the result of humility. The presentation of the Messiah here is of One who is humble. This thought originated in some *trait* which was borrowed from Tradition, but the original meaning of which had been lost. In Jeremiah xvii. 25, xxii. 4, it is emphasized how that the future king will make his entry in majesty and magnificence, with chariots and horses, as beseems a mighty and victorious ruler. Only from the time of Solomon were horses introduced into the country on a large scale, but their use was restricted to kings and to the nobility. The poor had to content themselves with donkeys. When,

THE MESSIANIC ERA A TIME OF PEACE

therefore, the Messiah is represented as riding upon an ass, it would in later times have been regarded as a sign of humility. But while this *explanation* is new, the *trait* itself was old. In earlier times, and even into the days of the monarchy, the ass was ridden by princes (Judg. x. 4; xii. 14; 2 Sam. xix. 27)."[1] There can be no question that this *trait* of humility in the Messiah is very striking when contemplated without reference to Christ's entry into Jerusalem, as is so often done; the significance of it lies, as it seems to the present writer, in the fact that it is intended to emphasize the *peaceful* character of the Messianic Era, which is the note sounded throughout the passage.

In the passages considered above, therefore, the adaptation of the earlier myth-material is seen in the fact that as the " Golden Age " was above all conceived of as a time of peace, so the Messianic Era has as its chief characteristic *peace*. The development of this thought is seen in that it is not merely peace as opposed to warfare that is to be enjoyed in the Messianic Era, but also the peace that is the lot of those who keep God's judgments and walk in His ways. This " peace of God," in its supremest development and in its highest spiritual form, is described in the sublime words: *Behold, the tabernacle of*

[1] *Op. cit.* p. 287.

THE EVOLUTION OF THE MESSIANIC IDEA

God is with men, and he shall dwell with them, and they shall be his peoples, and God himself shall be with them; and he shall wipe away every tear from their eyes; and death shall be no more; neither shall there be mourning, nor crying, nor pain, any more (Rev. xxi. 3, 4).

2. Another leading characteristic of the Golden Age was happiness and contentment. It is necessary to emphasize wherein, according to the earlier conceptions, this happiness, and consequent contentment, lay. It was entirely of a materialistic character; it will not be necessary to quote passages to show this, several have already been referred to in earlier chapters, and moreover, the point is fairly obvious. It will be sufficient to say that, according to early ideas, men who lived during the " Golden Age " would be happy and contented because, besides peace— which has already been referred to—they would have food and drink in abundance, the land would yield its increase, and it would be a time of perpetual rest. These ideas were adapted and became more and more spiritualized; a few examples of this may be given; Isaiah lv. 1-3: *Ho, every one that thirsteth, come ye to the waters; and he that hath no money come buy and eat; yea, come, buy wine and milk without money and without price. Wherefore do ye weigh out money for that which is not bread? And your earnings for that*

THE MESSIANIC ERA A TIME OF HAPPINESS

which is not satisfying? Hearken diligently unto me, and eat that which is good, and let your soul delight itself with fatness. Incline your ear and come unto me; hear, and your soul shall live; and I will make an everlasting covenant with you, the sure mercies of David. This spiritualizing of ideas that were originally of a wholly materialistic character is further illustrated by the following passage: *And in this holy mountain shall Jahwe of hosts make for all the peoples a feast of fat things, a feast of wines upon the lees, of fat things full of marrow, of wines upon the lees well-strained* (Isa. xxv. 6). Originally, words of this kind must unquestionably have been understood in a literal sense—Cheyne refers to the passage as descriptive of " a splendid feast of coronation "—but the prophet is utilizing ancient material, and adapting it, and in his mouth they cannot have been used literally; any doubt about this is set at rest by considering the context, v. 8: *He hath swallowed up death for ever; and the Lord Jahwe shall wipe away tears from off all faces* (cf. Rev. xxi. 4, quoted above); *and the reproach of his people shall he take away from off all the earth; for Jahwe hath spoken it.* Quotations to the same effect need not be multiplied; the spiritualizing process was bound to come with the gradual growth of spiritual perception among the Israelite teachers. The ancient idea reached its highest point of spiritual adaptation in the beautiful words of the Apocalyptist: *They shall hunger no more, neither thirst any more; neither shall the sun strike upon them, nor any heat; for the Lamb which is in the midst of the throne shall be their shepherd, and shall guide them unto fountains of waters of life; and God shall wipe away every tear from their eyes* (Rev. vii. 16, 17).

III.

There are, finally, three other points, of a minor character, two of which serve to illustrate the way in which the ancient myth-material concerning the " Golden Age " was adapted and spiritualized for the purposes of higher teaching in reference to the Messianic Era, while the other is an interesting instance of the fundamental idea being retained in its new environment; these deserve a brief notice.

1. We have seen above that the *scene* of the " Golden Age " was conceived of as being located upon a mountain; this is called the " Mount of God" or " Mount of Jahwe," sometimes it is also referred to as the " Garden of God." Originally the actual situation of this divine domain was vaguely pointed to as being in the north; later on the exact limits of the garden were described (Gen. ii. 8 ff.). A specific Israelite development,

THE "MOUNT OF JAHWE"

in later times, transferred this mountain to Jerusalem, and Mount Zion was spoken of as " God's hill," where He dwelt (see the various references given above). This conception was then brought into connexion with the Messianic Era ; but, generally speaking, the rule of the Messiah upon this mountain was taken in a literal sense. In a passage like Isaiah ii. 2-4, based as it is on pre-existing material, it is possible that with the literal sense more spiritual ideas were intermixed, —and this applies to some other passages ; but, as a rule, it is clear that a belief in the literal fulfilment as to the locality of the Messiah's kingdom was held. This is a belief which in the Old Testament was never really spiritualized. In post-Biblical Judaism the Hellenistic Jews were much occupied in teaching a "transcendental Messianism," and were deeply interested in speculative schemes regarding the "end" of the age, and all that such involved; but according to the teaching of official Judaism there was, right through the earlier centuries of the Christian Era, a distinction between the idea of the " Kingdom of Heaven," a spiritual kingdom over which God reigns, and the kingdom of Israel reigned over by the Messiah, which was a purely earthly kingdom. Later on, it is true, these two ideas became confused.[1] In the Old Testament, however,

[1] Cf. Oesterley and Box, *op. cit.* pp. 211, 212.

THE EVOLUTION OF THE MESSIANIC IDEA

the ancient idea of the ruler coming to rule upon his " mountain " holds good all through. This is an interesting example of an old-world idea continuing to exist in its literal sense in spite of the fact that so many of the ideas closely connected with it became spiritualized.

2. But an instance of another kind is that of the " Waters of Life." In Genesis ii. 10 (cf. i. 6) we read of the " river that went out of Eden to water the garden " ; on Babylonian analogy this river contained the waters of life.[1] That this idea of the Waters of Life was familiar among the Israelites is clear from a number of passages, e.g. Psalm xxxvi. 10 (9) : *For with thee is the fountain of life*; Psalm xlvi. 5 (4) : *A river (there is), its streams make glad the city of God*; Psalm lxv. 10 (9) : *The river of God is full of water*;[2] more striking is perhaps the passage Ezekiel xlvii. 1–12 —we read here of the waters which came forth from under the Temple, and went on increasing as they flowed, and when they came to the sea the waters of the sea were healed : *And it shall come to pass that every living creature which swarmeth in every place whither the river comes shall live* . . . (verse 9) ; see also Zechariah xiv. 8 : *And it shall come to pass in that day that living waters shall*

[1] Schrader KAT (3rd ed.), pp. 523 ff.
[2] The difference of the words, in Hebrew, used in these passages does not affect the underlying idea, which is identical in each case.

go out from Jerusalem. Here, then, we have the original Waters of Life, conceived of as flowing in the abode of the gods, adapted to Israelite conceptions. At first, probably, the belief was concerned with material waters which would flow from the mount of God in the happy time to come; then, as for example in the Zechariah passage, this was adapted to the Messianic Era. In later times the idea became one which was purely spiritual, as in Revelation xvii. 7: *For the Lamb which is in the midst of the throne shall be their shepherd, and shall guide them unto fountains of waters of life;* again, in xxii. 1: *And he showed me a river of water of life, bright as crystal, proceeding out of the throne of God . . .;* so, too, in verse 17 of the same chapter: *And he that is athirst let him come; he that will, let him take the water of life freely.*

3. Very closely connected with the idea of the "Waters of Life" is that of the "Tree of Life." The belief in the "Tree of Life" is one of the most widely diffused that exist; and therefore, although Babylonian influence in this, as in so much else, played its part among the Israelites, there is no reason to believe that the Israelites themselves were without some independent ideas of their own on this point. In the garden of Eden, we read, there was a Tree of Life; Jahwe is represented as fearing lest the man should eat of this tree, and live for ever;

therefore he is driven out of the garden, and the Cherubim are placed there " to keep the way of the tree of life " (Gen. iii. 22-24; cf. ii. 9). We have seen above that there are parallels for the idea of such a tree growing in the garden of the gods. This tree was evidently conceived of as one of the most remarkable features in the " Garden of Jahwe," which, as already remarked, was the scene of the time of happiness long ago, and which was also to be the scene of the return of the " Golden Age." [1] In Ezekiel xlvii. 12, we read: *And by the river, upon its banks, on either side, shall grow every tree for food, whose leaf shall not wither, neither shall its fruit fail; every month shall it bear its firstfruits, because its waters come forth out of the sanctuary, therefore their fruit shall be for food, and their leaves for healing* (cf. xxviii. 13, xxxiii. 3 ff.); that this was in the " garden of God " is clear from the fact that the waters issued from the sanctuary, which was situated upon the " mountain of God "—the " garden " and the " mountain of God " being synonymous. In the Genesis passage the description is meant to be taken literally; in Ezekiel the thought of life-giving trees is adapted and utilized in his vision of the future. But as in the case of the " Waters of Life," so with the " Tree of Life," its full spiritual

[1] Cf. the extremely interesting—and, from the present point of view, important—passage: 4 Esdr. viii. 52-54.

THE "TREE OF LIFE"

development is found in the Apocalypse : *To him that overcometh, to him will I give to eat of the tree of life, which is in the Paradise of God* (ii. 7) ; *And on this side of the river and on that was the tree of life, bearing twelve crops of fruit, yielding its fruit every month ; and the leaves of the tree were for the healing of the nations* (xxii. 2) ; and, once more : *Blessed are they that wash their robes, that they may have the right to come to the tree of life, and may enter in by the gates into the city* (xxii. 14).

* * *

It is thus both in the main idea as well as in details that a process of adaptation and development may be seen to have been at work. Lines of demarcation are, of course, not to be looked for, material and spiritual beliefs must have merged the one into the other for many a generation before a really definite differentiation could have become apprehended. For this reason clear steps in the development cannot be pointed out ; all that is possible is to indicate the fact of such development ; and this, it may be hoped, the examples given above have done.

CHAPTER XVII.

CONCLUSION.

We have attempted to give some reasons for believing that the leading conceptions comprised under the term *Messianism*, in the widest sense in which this word can be employed, go back in germ to the earliest dawn of the human understanding. Within the compass of a single volume it has manifestly been impossible to deal in any way exhaustively with such a vast subject; unfortunately, such partial treatment must necessarily result in a somewhat inadequate presentation of the argument; this is, however, inevitable when the subject covers such a wide area in its various ramifications. But the central thoughts which have been emphasized in the preceding pages have, it is hoped, been put with sufficient clearness. These we must now very briefly summarize.

Certain elemental characteristics in primitive man were, in course of time, expressed articulately in the form of *myths*, *i.e.*, the pictorial representation of ideas. These ideas, which arose in the mind of early man and which were clothed in the realistic garb of myths, witness to what was at

CONCLUSION

one time in the history of mankind the normal method of divine inspiration; for it is difficult to conceive of any other way whereby the knowledge of eternal truths could be brought home to the minds of men in a primitive stage of culture. The *form* of these myths was determined by the elemental human emotions of fear, the sense of dependence, and the desire to be happy; and in the divine economy they were employed in order to prepare and fit men's minds for the reception of abiding truths—truths which were to become more and more apprehended as the ages went on.

These myths were, for convenience' sake, called the "Tehom-Myth," the "*Heilbringer-*" or "Jahwe-Myth," and the "Golden Age-" or "Paradise-Myth," which corresponded to the three elemental human characteristics just referred to. It was held that, owing to the way in which these myths originated, it was natural to suppose that they arose, in very varying forms, all the world over, and that there was therefore no reason to postulate single prototypes. This supposition received some justification from the examples given of the existence of these myths among many very different peoples in many parts of the world widely separated geographically.

From this it followed that in ancient literatures, such as that contained in the Old Testament, traces of these myths might not only reasonably be looked for, but ought from the nature of the case to be plainly discernible; examples of such traces in the Old Testament were then given with the object of showing that this was actually the case.

But among a people like the Israelites, in whom the religious sense was so strikingly and uniquely developed, it could not fail but that teachers would be forthcoming who would, through divine guidance, perceive in these myths elements which were infinitely more significant than earlier ages could ever have conceived them to be; for they contained the germs of eternal truths which could only be realized by men in whom the faculty for apprehending spiritual truth was more fully developed than could have been the case in those earlier stages of human culture. These Israelite teachers, therefore, utilized this floating myth-material and adapted it to higher teaching.

It was, further, pointed out that, in accordance with this evolutionary process, the "*Tehom*-Myth" developed finally into the belief in Satan as the personification and embodiment of all evil. The "*Heilbringer*-Myth" presented a more complicated history; the characteristics of the "Saviour-Hero" were in course of time transferred to Jahwe, who was at first conceived of as fulfilling the functions which in later times, and

CONCLUSION

with certain modifications, were applied to the Messiah; but, according to the further and more developed teaching of the prophet Isaiah, Jahwe and the Messiah were to be wholly differentiated, while the inseparable connexion between them was shown to have been the unique outpouring of the Spirit of Jahwe upon the Messiah. Although the point is not referred to above, as being outside the scope of the present enquiry, this Isaianic teaching cannot have failed to suggest an adumbration of the Christian doctrine of the Holy Trinity. Then, further, the " Golden Age- " or " Paradise-Myth " was shown to have consisted of two complementary parts, one dealing with the past, the other looking forward to the future; and it was held that the belief concerning the Messianic Era to come was ultimately based upon the latter part of this myth.

The great cycle of truths, including both their origins and developments, comprised within the subject-matter referred to, constitute the content of the comprehensive term " Messianic Idea."

Into the further evolution of these truths no attempt was made to enter, because the investigation was primarily concerned with the Old Testament. But it is obvious that the whole subject has the closest possible bearing upon Christian

THE EVOLUTION OF THE MESSIANIC IDEA

belief; and the three words: *Sin, Saviour, Salvation*, comprise the essence of the truths, in process of being unfolded, with which the foregoing pages have been occupied. So that the final conclusion to be drawn from what has been said is that in these myths some of the central truths of Christianity were potentially in existence at the time when men first began to be thinking beings.

To the minds of some the study of Religion on the comparative method has resulted in showing that Christianity is merely a link, and nothing more, in the long chain of human thought and aspiration, and that it is superior to other forms of religion simply because it is the latest and most developed of these; and in support of such contentions it is pointed out that all Christian doctrine is to be discerned in germ and in process of development in earlier forms of belief, and that therefore Christianity cannot claim to be a religion *sui generis*. Such an Essay as the foregoing would doubtlessly be described as an illustration of the truth of their contention by those who hold this view. But the present writer maintains that a wholly different attitude may be taken up in regard to this matter, an attitude which he believes to be at least as justifiable as that just referred to; and so far from the argument of the foregoing pages being one which tends to discredit the

CONCLUSION

truths of Christianity, he contends that the exact reverse is the case. The point of view from which one approaches the discussion of a difficult subject like this must to a very large extent decide the attitude taken up in regard to it ; but since this applies to both the apologist and the antagonist, neither has any right to find fault with the acknowledged predisposition of the other. To this it will, of course, be retorted that the proper, the scientific, way of approaching the subject is to do so *without* predisposition, and with a wholly open mind. The present writer trusts he may be forgiven for expressing his conviction that this is an absolute impossibility. If the facts of the case on either side could be placed before one whose previous education, training and mode of thought had been such as to have permitted him to have remained uninfluenced by either pro-Christian or anti-Christian tendencies—a thing in itself quite unthinkable—then it would be possible for such a man to approach this subject without a predisposition in favour of Christianity or antagonistic to it—in a word, with an open mind. But with all the intention and desire in the world to be unbiassed in deciding the justice or otherwise of the two rival schools of thought referred to above, it is impossible, in the nature of things, for a man to divest himself of the previous tendencies which his up-bringing has created when he sets himself to enquire into the claims of these two schools of thought. It is a different thing altogether when the study has been entered upon ; then facts may, and probably will, cause preconceived notions to be modified, and perhaps altered ; the Christian believer may find that his faith receives some severe shocks, the sceptic may be brought to realize that Christian truth is much wider and more far-reaching than he could have believed before. But what is maintained here is that it is impossible to *approach* the question as to whether Christianity is only a development of earlier forms of belief, and therefore not what it claims to be, or whether because Christianity is true therefore all earlier forms of belief contained scintillations of truth and were gradually converging towards the Absolute Truth contained in Christianity—it is impossible to *approach* this question without a predisposition in favour of one side or the other. It is for this reason that the writer maintains that an attitude wholly different from that of the anti-Christian school of thought is at least as justified as this, in spite of the fact that his pro-Christian attitude in interpreting the facts under consideration is frankly acknowledged. That attitude may be expressed in very few words. To Christians the existence of Sin is a thing so painfully obvious that to them its denial, according to some " modern " theories

CONCLUSION

which suggest the idea of *réchauffé*, only emphasizes its prevalence. The universal prevalence of Sin, according to Christian belief, and the acknowledgement of man's impotence in facing it unaided, compel him to look to a Saviour Who can help him, as no one else can, to overcome it ; and this victory over Sin through the Saviour, brings with it hereafter eternal salvation. These beliefs are held by all Christians to be *living* truths, and as such must have existed from the beginning of the world ; if they were not so apparent in earlier days as they are now, it was simply because men were incapable of apprehending them ; but the point insisted on is that they were there, otherwise there could be no question of their *evolution*, which is the fact which the foregoing pages have attempted to point out. Since, therefore, these beliefs of Christianity are of the nature of eternal truths, earlier forms of faith which contained adumbrations of them were, to that extent, themselves true.

The real difference between the two schools of thought referred to above lies here ; according to the one, Christianity is not what it claims to be because it is the lineal descendant of primitive forms of belief ; according to the other, primitive forms of belief contained elements of truth because the evolution of these truths shows that they form part of the Christian faith. On the one hand, it is maintained that because the antecedents are false therefore the final development which is based upon them is also false ; on the other, that because the development is true therefore the antecedents must also partake of truth. The present writer's attitude in face of these alternatives, to repeat what was said above, is as follows: " So far from the antecedents, on account of their inadequateness and incompleteness, being used for impugning the reality of the truth in its developed form, may one not be rather justified in recognizing elements of the truth in the former on account of the proved truth of the latter ? Because an acorn does not exhibit the trunk, root, branches and leaves of an oak, it is not therefore not potentially an oak ; rather, just because we know the latter in its completeness, we are justified in seeing in the former, potentially, all that the latter contains."

The study of Comparative Religion must in the future become one of the greatest dangers to the Christian religion, or else its handmaiden ; if the former, then Christian Apologetics will have to find new defensive armour, but if the latter, then its offensive armour will have become stronger than ever.

If God is from everlasting, then Truth which is, as we believe, from God must have been from everlasting too ; and in this case the history of

CONCLUSION

mankind has borne witness, in a halting and inadequate manner it may be, but upon the whole according to the best of its ability, to things which had within them the germ of Truth. And if there is any truth at all in the "Messianic Idea," in that wide sense in which this expression has here been used, then the fact that it has gone through a process of Evolution proves that elements of truth were contained within its antecedents from the very beginning.

THE END.

www.ingramcontent.com/pod-product-compliance
Lightning Source LLC
Chambersburg PA
CBHW050339230426
43663CB00010B/1923